The Million Dollar Secret
Hidden
in Your Mind

D0913676

Every man who knows how to read has it in his power to magnify himself, to multiply the ways in which he exists, to make his life full, significant, and interesting.
—ALDOUS HUXLEY

The Million Dollar Secret Hidden in Your Mind

Anthony Norvell

BARNES & NOBLE BOOKS

A DIVISION OF HARPER & ROW, PUBLISHERS

New York, Hagerstown, San Francisco, London

I dedicate this book to my thousands of Carnegie Hall lecture members and students.

They have learned how to use the principles given in this book, and their lives reflect the success, health, happiness, and financial prosperity that this book offers those who seriously study its message.

Introduction

At some time in your life you have probably thought, "If I only had a million dollars I would be the happiest person in the world!"

It's true that money would help you achieve material comforts and give you a sense of security you do not now have.

But there are things in life that money cannot buy worth more than a million dollars: peace of mind, health, true friends, love, happiness and spiritual fulfillment are treasures beyond price.

In giving you the formula for achieving riches, I include all these other values as well as money and its material equivalents. The million dollar consciousness you will build through this study will show you how to have money and be happy. Many millionaires who stress only money are not happy in other areas of their lives. Hetty Green, a famous miser worth one hundred million dollars, lived in a cold water flat, wore shabby clothes, and begged for free food from restaurants, where she pretended to be poor. With all her millions this unfortunate woman was more poverty stricken than the poorest person.

How I Discovered the Million Dollar Secret

I have spent many years studying the laws and principles used by the most successful men and women of history. I have investigated the lives of geniuses, millionaires, titans of industry, writers, composers, bankers, financiers, actors, and producers, and I discovered that they all used the million dollar secret formula that I am revealing to you in this book.

The inventions, dscoveries, formulas, business ideas and new products which they used are lying like golden nuggets on the surface of your consciousness, waiting to be discovered. Scientists now say that since the dawn of the atomic and electronic age there are literally thousands of new products to be invented. Your chances of making a fortune will be even greater in the future, if you are mentally fortified with the knowledge that is available in this book.

Many Facets to the Million Dollar Secret

This knowledge may be applied in many ways. If you wish to use it to learn how to achieve a vast fortune, you may do so.

If you wish to release new mental gifts and add greater stature to your intellect, you will find the method for doing so here. One creative idea can make you a million dollars. The man who invented the can opener made a fortune. Someone thought of the mercury switch to turn lights on and off, and he made millions. The men and women who write great songs, novels, poems, and television or motion picture scripts often make fortunes. So do people like Helena Rubenstein, Elizabeth Arden, and Charles Revson of Revlon, who give beauty to the world.

The secret power back of all great fortunes is creative intelligence. You can convert nature's resources or your own mental energies into money or its equivalents.

Money Is Not Everything

In studying this million dollar secret formula keep in mind that money is not everything. Our country is the richest nation in the world and yet we have not solved all our problems. To help overcome these problems we need other values; we need to be enriched mentally, emotionally, and spiritually. The true riches of life lie in the unseen realm of the mind and spirit.

In our modern age man has achieved greater things than at any other time in history. Through the genius of Einstein man learned how to split the atom and release power that will bring a new era of prosperity when atomic power is harnessed for peaceful pursuits instead of for war. Leonardo da Vinci's dream of the first airplane, paved the way for our modern spacemen to fly to the moon, land and safely return to earth. See the marvels that man has created in our own age: new fabrics, plastics, nylon, new metals for building, air conditioners, computers, electronics, radio, television, motion pictures, automobiles, space ships and a thousand and one other miracles that have changed the face of the world.

Yet, in our quest for the million dollar secret and the things money can buy, let us not blind ourselves to the true facts of our modern existence. Despite our greater material prosperity we still have not overcome war. We still have not learned how to master sickness. Half the beds in our hospitals are filled with the mentally ill, who break down under the pressures and strains of our modern age of chaos, noise, pollution and confusion.

We are still waging a battle with ecological problems. Our polluted air and the poisoning of our rivers, lakes and oceans with industrial wastes threatens our fish, birds and wildlife. Our forests are being denuded, our natural resources of oil, coal and iron are being depleted; our soil faces continued erosion, and man's greed and selfishness imperil the future of all of us.

The Secret Power Hidden in Your Mind

You can build the million dollar consciousness by using the secret power hidden in your mind. If your inner dream is one of health, happiness, popularity and social success, you can use this formula for achieving all these. The million dollar secret will reveal an inner kingdom of peace, poise and power that lies within the innermost recesses of your soul. You can learn to tune in on the highest and most inspiring thoughts of great men and women of history and have a million dollars worth of love, happiness and true enjoyment of life.

Yes, the million dollar secret combines mental, emotional and spiritual riches. You can be rich on all planes of consciousness and truly fulfill the great destiny that God intended for you.

A legend is told of the creation of the universe. The gods held a conference and one of them said, "Let us give to man the same creative power that we ourselves possess. Where shall we hide this priceless gift?"

Another answered, "Let us hide it where man will never think to look for it: within his own mind."

That is where the million dollar secret resides—within your own mind, your own consciousness. Here it is that you can find the creative power to build a material, monetary fortune and to find health, happiness, friendship, love, intellectual enjoyment and peace of mind.

Study the principles in this book carefully. Apply them to your everyday life and believe that the miracle of riches and abundance can happen to you, as it has to thousands of others. You will gradually become a living, walking symbol of the power and might that is in the million dollar secret that lies hidden within your mind.

Contents

1

Dynamic Thinkers Rule
the World

The human mind is one of the greatest instruments in the world. Man's thinking shapes the world in which he lives. Through dynamic mind-power man has been able to conceive and create such marvels as space ships, jet planes, radio, television, and atomic power. It is dynamic thinking that has achieved this greatness for man. His vision and daring have caused him to reach out into time and space and attempt to reach the stars. He has already walked on the moon and now is aiming at Mars and other planets in our solar system.

Inconceivable power resides in your mind when it is released from the shackles of fear and limitation. You live in an unlimited universe where there is unlimited power. When you learn how to expand your consciousness and release dynamic mind power, you can achieve things that you never dreamed were possible before.

Power-Potentials of Genius

Throughout history certain men and women have shown themselves capable of leading others to glory and achievement. These people seemed to possess some strange inner quality that made them outstanding. They had a dynamic quality in their personalities that made them magnetic and forceful. They seemed to possess an intuitive power that was amazing. They knew things that others were ignorant of. They had the courage and daring to attempt seemingly impossible things and they usually attained the goals they set for themselves.

Such men and women throughout history were called geniuses. They had energy and purposefulness and an inner drive that pushed them unerringly towards a great destiny. The secret power that these great people used is still in existence today. The greatness of their achievements may be duplicated by anyone who has the necessary knowledge. If you probe the power-potentials of your own mind, you can startle the world with your creative gifts.

The dynamic mind-power of a Leonardo da Vinci, who created such magnificent paintings as The Last Supper and the Mona Lisa, may be yours. You may not paint great pictures, but you can use the same creative power da Vinci used in your own particular field. The same creative power may be used to build skyscrapers and bridges that geniuses have used to paint, compose or write imperishable works of art.

The vision of a Columbus is still in existence in the universe. You may tap the power Columbus used and discover new worlds in industry, finance, science, invention and the arts.

You have the same identical brain cells as Shakespeare had. You may not write great literature, but you can divert this dynamic mind-power into other channels that will make you rich and famous.

Amazing Results through Dynamic Thinking

When the principles of Dynamic Thinking are applied, it is amazing what results can be achieved. Throughout my years of lecturing in world-famous Carnegie Hall, I have observed many ordinary men and women, who did extraordinary things when they once unlocked the tremendous reserves of power within their own minds.

Here are just a few results observed in some of these students.

A young man, who had failed as an actor, came to our lectures and received this training on mental power. He became inspired to go into sales work for a big insurance company. The first year he made more money than his combined salary had been for three previous years. He had never had any training for sales work before.

A cowboy from Texas came to our classes and studied the principles given in this book. He decided to become a hair stylist. In four years time he was making $30,000 a year teaching high styling before large audiences who paid him $80.00 each for the advanced course. He also published a book, which he illustrated, on hair styling. He won every national and international trophy on hair styling, an inconceivable achievement! From cowboy to leading hair stylist. No one would believe such a transformation unless he could see it. And yet, it's true. This is one of the miracles that can take place when you apply principles of dynamic thinking that lead to dynamic action.

Muscle Man Makes Good

A muscle man who studied these principles with me back in Hollywood, when I was doing a series of lectures there, was shaken out of his lethargy by dynamic thinking. He went to Rome and made a picture called, *Hercules*. This picture grossed fifteen million dollars, and the star, Steve Reeves, now gets half a million dollars for each picture. Dynamic thinking changed him from a boy no studio in Hollywood wanted, to a new, dynamic and forceful personality that could command such a large salary.

A young lady who was a manicurist, studied these principles and heard me say in one lecture, "What hast thou in thine house?" She had studied manicuring, but her ambitions were way beyond the limited scope and salary of such a profession. She had a dream of sailing around the world, of marrying, having a beautiful home and a glamorous social life. She began to apply the principles she learned. Her higher mind led her to a contact that brought her a job as a manicurist on a round-the-world-cruise ship. On this cruise she met a man who fell in love with her. She married him on board ship, and later discovered he was rich. Today she is living in a luxurious home, and is a social leader in her community.

A young man came to these lectures, also in Hollywood, who was a real estate salesman, with a minor success. Through the inspiration he received from this work, he branched out into his own office a few years ago and now has fourteen salesmen working for him. He is one of the biggest real estate brokers on the west coast.

This power of dynamic thinking which can change your world for you, is not limited to the young, or to men only. A woman past fifty who applied these principles, was inspired to study stenotype operating. Everyone told her no one would hire a woman of her age, but she had absolute confidence that what she was doing was right. She got a job immediately after graduating as secretary to a leading judge, and her salary was over $200 a week.

I could give you literally hundreds of illustrations of men and women who have applied the principles of dynamic thinking and who have achieved great things because they had the courage to dare and do.

You were born to be great; to have the things that make you happy. You are only as limited as your thinking. Change your thinking from that which is weak and indecisive, to that which is powerful and dynamic, and you will see astounding results in your life.

Many people say, "But everything's been discovered and invented. How can I possibly do anything new or different?" To such people I can only say that in this dynamic decade ahead, man will still achieve some of the greatest things that have ever been evolved for humanity. Men and women, like you who are studying the principles given in this book, will break through the limitations of your circumstances and surroundings, and achieve great things in many fields.

Conrad Hilton's Formula for Success

I talked to Conrad Hilton once at a party at my home in Bel Air, California. Some of the country's leading society figures were there; men and women who had achieved great things in industry, the arts, and finances. I asked Hilton for his success formula in a few words. He said, "When I owned a small hotel early in my career, and failed, I decided I had been thinking in too limited a sphere. I decided it was just as easy for me to think in terms of big things, as to think of only accomplishing small things. I began to visualize a big chain of hotels, and found it was as easy to think of a big chain as to think of only one. I began to think in terms of big money, and decided it takes no more energy to think of one million dollars than to think of one dollar. A million is only one, with six zeros attached."

Geniuses of History

It takes dynamic thinking to give you the mental power to blast off into the stratosphere of greatness and success. You have the same brain cells, the same muscles, nerves, and heart that the great geniuses of history had. It is the mental power that you send hustling through those muscles and nerves, to that heart, which causes you to rise to a higher level on the ladder of dreams.

Many people are afraid to try their mental wings. They have to be pushed by circumstances into positions of power and greatness. I claim that every person is an undiscovered genius, if he can only learn how to release the dynamic power that lies within his own mind. Science says that there is enough atomic energy in a single lead pencil to blow up a city the size of New York. The atomic power that can drive you to amazing heights of achievement resides in the secret convolutions of your brain. When you once learn how to channel this power in the right way, you can achieve anything your heart desires.

Believe in Your Dream

Take from history the astounding accomplishments of Joan of Arc. Here was a simple, peasant girl of France. She had no great skill, no education, no physical power. She saw visions and heard voices. She dreamed that she would one day lead the armies of France to victory. When she revealed this dream to others, they thought she was deluded and laughed her to scorn. Others thought she was mad. Finally she convinced one of the rulers that she could achieve victory for France. She led the armies to amazing victories, in the face of overwhelming odds.

What was Joan of Arc's secret power? She believed in her dream. She had the dynamic vision that motivated her to seek the means to victory. She saw herself doing the great deeds. Some strange, intuitive power within her mind forced her to seek out a great destiny. This amazing woman, who believed in her dream, was later sainted. A truly great achievement for one who sprang from such lowly surroundings!

You are only able to achieve that which you can conceive. If you believe in your dream, have faith in this inner power of your mind, it will release dynamic mental energy that will lead you to your high goal.

I Think, therefore I Am

The famous philosopher Descartes, had a philosophy which may be summarized in one dynamic sentence: "I think, therefore I am."

Dynamic thinking can set into motion a series of reactions that are cataclysmic in their effects.

Ask yourself: "What do I think?" Then answer candidly.

Do you think of yourself as being a failure in life?

Do you think you are inferior and inadequate?

Do you think you are doomed to poverty all your life?

Do you think your personality is unattractive?

If you are thinking the above negative thoughts, you are short-circuiting the dynamic power of your brain and creating the image of these negative conditions in the outer circumstances of your life. Thoughts are a psychological reality. We each live in a world colored and dominated by our own private thought atmosphere.

Change the picture of your thoughts from negative to positive. Dynamic thinking will cause you to **be** that which you **think.**

Think you are successful.

Think that you are adequate, that you are equal to others.

Think that you can achieve the riches others have.

Think that your personality may become magnetic and attractive. You are using the magical power of dynamic thinking in the moment that you think in a positive manner. "I think, therefore I am." Write that down on a card which you can consult several times daily, and on that card write, "I think and talk success, health, happiness and achievement. I think great thoughts, therefore I am great."

Unlimit Your Thinking

As you unlimit your thinking and begin to expand your consciousness, you will release tremendous mental power that can cause you to achieve the seemingly impossible.

When Jules Verne wrote his *Around the World in Eighty Days* it was considered a daring and impossible concept. Now man has circled the earth in eighty minutes in his space ship. What a difference in time! What a difference in mental concepts! When you unlimit your thinking you can break through the barriers of time and space and overcome the limitations of poverty, lack of education, age, and other negative conditions that may impede your progress.

With the splitting of the atom, scientists released a new and tremendous source of power for the world to use. This atomic power is within man's mind also. When you learn how to tap this inner, vital life-force, you may shape events to fit your needs. You may achieve anything you can conceive.

It was the dynamic thinking of men's minds that first conceived the splitting of the atom, the building of the first space ship, the harnessing of electricity to do great work, the imprisoning of that electricity in a bulb to turn night into day. Man's mind conceived and built the motor car, the jet plane, the modern radio and television.

Be an Explorer in the Dimension of Mind

The daring explorations of Columbus were so bold in concept that they changed the history of the entire world. It took Columbus sixty-seven days to cross the Atlantic in 1492. Now man crosses the same ocean in a few hours time in his jet planes. What is the difference? It's the same ocean, the same time and space is involved. There is only one difference: Man's concept of time has changed. He has accelerated his thinking in relation to his world, and, consequently the world has seemingly shrunk in size. Man's mind has bridged the gap between thought and reality. He reached for the moon in his thinking, and he found the means to get there! What man can conceive, he may achieve. Dare to be an explorer in the dimension of mind, and you will be able to close the gap between your inner dream and reality. You can do this quickly, more quickly than people who do not know this secret of dynamic thinking.

Dare to Think Great Thoughts

Dare to think great thoughts. The nature of your thoughts determines the character you build, and your character in turn, determines the experiences that shape your future destiny. Your thinking each day should encompass success, fame, fortune, health, and power, and soon, as you indulge these thoughts more and more, your character will begin to reflect these things. You will become daring, courageous and bold enough to forge the means to achieve the dream you hold within your mind.

When you think that you are too old or too young to do great things, or that you are uneducated, poor, physically unattractive, or any other negative thought, you paralyze the power of your mind at its source and are unable to act in a bold, courageous manner.

When you change the pattern of your thinking to the positive side, you instantly release mental and physical forces that motivate your whole life in a positive direction. Think each day, when you arise, a group of positive thoughts, that will condition your mind and body for that entire day's action. These thoughts may be thought silently or said aloud as you make up, shave, or dress. The main thing is to **believe** what you are saying, for when you have faith in what you are thinking and doing, it sets up positive currents of energy in your brain and body and makes your thoughts and actions more dynamic and powerful.

Here is the regime of thinking you should indulge every morning when you arise.

"I am happy. I am healthy. I am successful. I will achieve big things today. I will make friends of everyone I meet today. I will be cheerful and optimistic. I have faith in myself and my co-workers. I am rich in the possession of good health, sanity, and all the free gifts of life. I enjoy life, and live it more fully. I am aware of the beauty about me. The sunshine, beauty of nature, the public parks, all these things I shall enjoy today, and share with the world. I am perfect."

You are shaping your thinking when you make such positive statements, in the direction of dynamic action. Psychologists have determined that we set the mental stage with our thoughts first, and then our bodies and our destinies reflect these thoughts.

"As a man thinketh in his heart, so is he."

"I think, therefore I am."

Two statements; one from the Bible, the other from a famous philosopher, but both meaning the same thing. You **become** that which you think most persistently and dynamically!

Six Rules for Building Dynamic Thinking

1. Sit down for ten minutes a day and try to think of something different and original about your own work . . . such thoughts as, how you might make changes; ways of better approach to selling your product, or new ways of doing the things that are now being done slowly or in a costly manner. In these ten minutes give your thoughts over completely to yourself and your thinking. Ask your-

self pertinent questions: Am I doing the best I can in my work? Do I have enough drive and aggressiveness? Am I too weak and vacillating in my personality? Do I dwell too much on the negative things of life and not enough on the positive?

2. Mentally visualize yourself in situations where you are using dynamic thinking; such as, giving a speech before a large group of people on some subject you know; giving a sales talk to some employer in which you tell of your qualifications; presenting a case in court, in which you are trying to impress a jury with the right of your case.

3. Run positive and dynamic thoughts through your mind that build your character and set the habit patterns of dynamic thought. "I now act decisively in everything I do." "I project friendliness in my personality and win friends everywhere I go." "I love other people and they will react to my love with friendly actions." "I am on my way to greatness and I shall strive to be worthy of life's richest rewards."

4. Build your power of dynamic thinking by building your knowledge each day. Learn one new word a day and use it in your day's activities. Write a short, inspirational sentence, giving as clearly as possible your chief objective in life. Study the life of some great man and pick one point in his philosophy which you can apply to your own life. For example: Washington: Truth. Lincoln: Justice. Franklin: Thrift.

5. Before going to bed each night review your day and mentally change the actions of that day that displease you. If you did or said anything that reflected weakness, indecision, vacillation, disorder and inharmony, relive the scene and correct it mentally so your actions are positive and dynamic.

6. Read at least fifteen minutes a day from some book that presents an inspired or new thought, or some magazine, like the *Reader's Digest,* that presents examples of great deeds from the lives of modern men and women. If you can read at least one hour a day, do so, for reading gives your mind that sharp edge which it requires for dynamic thinking. It helps you arrange the facts you read in your subconscious mind, in such a manner that they may be called upon in the future when you might need them.

Test Your Mental Strength

1. Do you make your mind up rapidly?
2. Do you stick to your ideas in the face of persuasion?
3. When out with friends, do they turn to you for decisions as to what to do, or where to go?
4. Do your co-workers ask your advice about things?
5. Do you aspire to a high goal in life?
6. Do you refuse to give up in the face of repeated failures?
7. Do you emulate the thoughts and deeds of great men?
8. Do you refuse to worry about things you cannot help?
9. Have you conquered most of your fears?
10. Do you think positive thoughts, such as courage, faith, love and happiness, most of the time?

Grade yourself 10% for each Yes. 70% fair. 80% good. 90% excellent. 100% genius rating.

2

The Undiscovered Genius
within Your Mind

Potentially your mind is that of a genius. You have the same capacity as a Beethoven or an Einstein. Psychologists have proved that the average person could achieve the same great things that geniuses have, if they would just use as little as ten per cent more of their brain potential. Think of it! You have the genius to create greatness if you will but use ten per cent more of your brain potential than you now use. In fact, the great psychologist William James goes even further in his discovery of the human mind: he states that the greatest geniuses of history used *only* ten per cent of their brain potential!

Now this is an astounding statement, and promises you untold power if you can only release a small part of your brain potential. The thoughts and inspiration of a Leonardo da Vinci may be imprinted on your consciousness and act as a blueprint upon which to construct your new and greater destiny.

The insight of a Galileo, the daring of a Newton, may be emblazoned upon your conscious and subconscious minds, causing you to break through the barriers of ignorance and limitation that may be keeping you from winning high goals in life.

The imagination and audacity of a Benjamin Franklin, or an Edison, may cause you to discover priceless secrets of the universe, as they did when they discovered and harnessed electric power. You can harness the genius within your mind and find a whole new world of wonder and enchantment.

Grow Wings of the Imagination

You are an undiscovered genius, and when you grow wings of the imagination you may soar into unlimited realms of great achievement. Dare to think of yourself as being an extraordinary person, with great powers of the mind. You were created with an imagination that can cause you to think of yourself as being big, successful, rich, powerful—anything you desire can be imaged, and the wings of imagination will carry you aloft into that rarefied atmosphere of genius and greatness.

On the first sketch of a flying machine ever built by man, Leonardo da Vinci wrote these prophetic words: "Man shall grow wings." That first airplane which da Vinci built, actually glided a few feet, for it had no motor, but the church leaders of that day made him destroy his flying machine.

You must grow wings of the imagination if you wish to soar above the barriers of ignorance, superstition and hatred which shroud the lowlands of human limitation today. Man is aiming for the stars in his space ships today; you must also aim at the stars of idealism, beauty, truth, goodness and knowledge, if you wish to rise above the gravity pull of failure, fear, frustration and poverty.

Building New Habit Patterns

Habit patterns hold everyone of us in their powerful grip. Perhaps the undiscovered genius within your mind is being stifled even now by the old habit patterns you have set in the past. These habit patterns may be set in your childhood, by your own family. They may have told you to forget your dream of being successful, of becoming a great writer, artist, actor, business man. These negative thoughts lodge in your subconscious mind and short-circuit the dynamic energy of your mind and body.

You must begin today to build new habit patterns of thought that will release you from your prison house of negative actions. Just think what creatures of habit we really are. You reach down in the morning and automatically lace your shoes without giving it a thought, but when you first learned how to do this simple act, it was a real effort. You shave and shower, or make up automatically while your mind thinks of other things. Habit makes your movements unconscious and effortless. You sit at a typewriter for days and consciously write pages of letters like *;lkj asdf* or *awsedrf, ;olikuj,* and at first it is a great effort and requires tremendous concentration. Soon habit takes over and you are writing the most involved words and sentences as automatically as you breathe, without any effort.

Your new habit patterns must be carefully built so they will replace the old habit patterns of failure, sickness, misery, age and unhappiness that might have been put into your mind. You do this through a mental process that changes your concepts about yourself and life in general. You begin to think right now that you can achieve any goal you wish to attain. You begin to imitate the thoughts and inspirations of the great geniuses of history. We emulate their high ideals, we perform the inspiring acts that made them great; we duplicate the great deeds of others by following in their mental footsteps.

You Are an Heir to a Kingdom

The Bible tells us, "You are an heir to a kingdom." Believe this statement as being literally true. It will help give you courage and faith. It will instantly help you shatter the mould of negative thoughts that might have been implanted in your mind as a child. The Bible also states, "It is the Father's good pleasure to give you the kingdom." Believe this, and you will instantly begin to act and think and talk in a much more positive manner. You will realize that the world and all therein was created for **you** to use and enjoy.

You were created in the image and likeness of God. This spiritual belief will also help you realize that nothing but the best is good enough for one of God's highest forms of creation. When you fortify your mind with this type of faith you will instantly release all the stored-up dynamic energy of your brain and body, and it will carry you on to great heights of achievement.

Goethe said of thought:

"Sow a thought, reap a habit;
Sow a habit, reap a character,
Sow a character, reap a destiny."

Actually you build your future destiny thought by thought, and as these thoughts become more dynamic and perfect, they begin to shape your character and destiny in paths of greatness.

Planting the Positive Seeds in Your Mind

What are the positive seeds that you must plant in your mind, if you wish to achieve a great destiny?

By planting the seed of happiness, you begin to come into experiences that reflect pleasure and joy.

By planting the seed of riches, you begin to do the things that will attract more money and make you rich.

By planting the seed of success in your work, you will gradually evolve into your right work, or business, and achieve success in that field.

The Bible also gives this great psychological law for planting positive thoughts or seeds in the mind. It says, "As ye sow so shall ye reap."

Build the habit patterns of thinking health, happiness, success, friendship, romance, riches, in your daily life. Each day when you are tempted to think depressing and dark thoughts of failure, sickness, age, accident, and hatred, change the trend to the positive side, and build the habit patterns that are positive and constructive. Soon you will find that it is impossible to let your mind dwell on moodiness, depression and negativity.

Charles Schwab's Secret

Charles Schwab, who made over a hundred million in his lifetime, knew well the secret power that can come from building habit patterns of positive thinking. He once said, "I have failed forty-nine per cent of the time and succeeded only fifty-one per cent of the time." That two per cent difference, if it is on the positive side, can spell the difference between success and failure.

You will undoubtedly experience many situations in life which you may put down as defeats. Actually, however, they are only life experiences common to all people. The only thing that really matters ultimately, is to have more of these positive, successful experiences, than those of defeat and failure. You can only do this by refusing to accept life's negative defeats as being real or permanent. Each time you suffer a reverse, come right back and try again, with the determination that this time you will really make the grade. Remember, there is only two per cent difference between failure and success. Think and live for that two per cent, not the other ninety-eight per cent of indifferent success.

Awaken the Mental Giant Slumbering within

Now you are embarked upon the thrilling voyage of discovery that will lead you to the finding of new worlds, but there are shoals and pitfalls which I must warn you about.

Most of the pitfalls are your own relatives and friends. They have lived with you for many years and they have been used to the shrinking violet you may have become under the regime of weak, negative thinking of the past. These friends and relatives feel comfortable in the presence of the small ego that fits their concept of your totality of power. When the slumbering mental giant that is within your mind, begins to stir restlessly and tries to shake off the chains that bind it to mediocrity, failure, poverty and ignorance, these people are apt to set up a clamor that will shock the giant back into his somnolent state of immobility and inertia.

These well-meaning souls will all scream as one, "You can't do it! You don't have the education to do great things. You're too old! You're too young! You were born on the other side of the railroad tracks." And, stunned by this clamor of deafening sound, the mental giant that is stirring within you may just yawn, stretch and go back into fitful slumber once again; a sleep of living death, with poverty, misery and unhappiness plaguing you the rest of your days.

Just remember, every genius of history had this same type of discouragement to go through, before breaking the bonds of negativity and frustration, and going on to heights of greatness. A prophet is without honor in his own country. Those closest to you sometimes are the very last ones to recognize the genius within you or to give you recognition for having great talent.

If He had Thought of It

Even such a great man as Columbus had to meet with this type of negativity and discouragement from those who opposed his daring dream. When he returned from his successful voyages, there were the grandees and nobles of the Court of Spain who were jealous of his accomplishments, and they tried to minimize his efforts.

At a royal banquet, honoring Columbus, the nobles made light of Columbus' great feat. When he saw their condescending and critical attitudes, Columbus asked that a raw egg be brought to him. Then he passed the egg around the table, asking if any of the nobles could make it stand on its end. Each tried and failed. The egg was passed back to Columbus and he tapped it on one end, and the egg stood on end perfectly.

One of the grandees remarked sarcastically, "Anyone could have done that, if he had thought of it!"

Columbus replied with a smile, "Yes, gentlemen, anyone could have proved that the world is round also, **if he had thought of it!**"

Your new worlds of discovery will suddenly appear on the horizon of your destiny when you begin to think them into being. The undiscovered genius within your mind is only awaiting your joyous discovery. Then it will gradually seek the means and the channel for the expression of its great ideas. If you really want to make a fortune, acquire some skill, achieve a great goal in life, you will find the means to do it. If you have a big enough vision, if you have faith in yourself and your goal, you can attain anything that you really want in life.

Steps to Take to Release the Undiscovered Genius within Your Mind

1. Each day try to originate some new and daring concept of thought in relation to your life. Write these down in a note book and begin to apply them to your activities.

2. Live in your imagination at least one half hour a day. See yourself as the person you wish to be. Visualize yourself as the manager of the department where you work. See yourself owning your own business. Imagine yourself taking trips to foreign countries. Build the new concept of your great powers by seeing how many refinements you can make on such inventions as the radio, television, typewriters, telephones. Write down ideas for great stories, novels, movies. You may not intend to be a writer but this mental exercise will extend your thinking to the realm of creative ideas and cause the subconscious mind to release more power to your everyday activities.

3. Pick some outstanding genius of history each day and emulate his philosophy, his thinking, his inspiration. Study the lives of the great geniuses of history, searching for these great thoughts which you may borrow and make a part of your own mental equipment. For instance, Pasteur. Concentrate on his persistence

and patience, and make it part of your mental equipment. Edison. Borrow his vision and curiosity, and apply those qualities to your own life, seeing how many things you can mentally create, and how many facts you can discover that are useful to you. Burbank. Borrow the trait that made him a genius. The love of beauty and a desire to create good for the world. Shakespeare. Borrow from this genius the beauty of words, and the highest form of cultural expression. If you take one genius a day, and apply his particular outstanding trait or quality to your own life, you will soon have such reflected power and glory, that you will become like the persons you have chosen as outstanding examples to emulate.

3

You Are Greater than
You Think

Most people have a tendency to minimize themselves and their abilities. Psychologists have tests that prove this. Such people depreciate their own talents, their personalities, and tend to put others on a pedestal.

You cannot achieve a great destiny or a big fortune, if you constantly believe yourself inferior and unworthy. Some people have subconscious feelings of guilt, put into their minds by their parents when they were children, and these guilt feelings hound them throughout life, making them unhappy, and dooming them to live lives that are inferior, poverty-stricken and inadequate. You have been told that it is wrong and sinful to want to be successful, famous and rich, and that only the "Meek shall inherit the earth." You must break such negativity at once, and believe that *you are greater than you think*.

Just stop and consider what an amazing life-intelligence resides within your brain. It is so great that it knows the secret for building the baby's body within the mother's womb in nine short months. It knows all the combinations of chemicals to create the hair, the nails, the complicated structure of the eye and the ear, the convolutions of your brain, all these amazing secrets are locked up within your own consciousness.

Tap the Power that Is Greater than You

This super-intelligence that resides within your mind is greater than you are. It knows how to mix the chemicals to create adrenalin, how to regulate your thyroid gland so it secretes just enough to keep the body functioning normally. It is the power that causes your brain to think and which stores up millions of sensations in the memory paths of your brain, so you can instantly refer to them when needed.

You can tap this amazing power that is greater than you. It is the Magic Genie within your mind, which can guide you to undreamed of heights of achievement.

Remember, the resourcefulness of this life force or intelligence that is in the universe is so great that it can cause a living organism to adapt itself to any condition or external environment. See how amazingly it works in nature. It produces different species in the animal kingdom, with different needs and functions. The elephant and the rhinoceros; the delicate humming bird and bee; the whale and the minnow. The entire universe operates under the impetus of this higher Universal Mind. You can learn to tap this power and channelize it to your own life needs.

This universal life force or intelligence knows how to create anything that you desire. It works within your mind, but it also works throughout nature, under laws that are as set and definite as the law of gravity.

In nature this intelligence grows shells to protect some of its creatures from extinction. It gives some animals and insects weapons to survive; the bee has its sting, the scorpion has its poison. It causes some to climb trees, others to live and breathe in water; it gives furry coats to the polar bear to survive in the arctic cold, and assures even a lazy bird like the cuckoo the right to survive. The cuckoo bird flies over the nests of other birds and mentally photographs the shape, size and color of the eggs in their nests, then it lays an egg in each nest that matches those already there. This lazy bird then flies away to enjoy itself while foster parents take care of its children!

What astounding power in that cuckoo causes it to duplicate other birds' eggs? Even science does not know the answer to that question, but a study of this strange bird made in England proves that it has some amazing intelligence that can cause it to do this miraculous feat.

The Unlimited World of Mind

This natural intelligence is greater in you than it is in all of nature's other creatures, for you represent the highest form of creation in the universe. When you discover the unlimited realm of the mind you can use it to shape the world you desire. This inner intuitive power that is in every animal, insect, bird and beast, is awaiting your recognition and bidding. When you once discover this power and learn through this study how to channelize it correctly, you will be able to achieve seeming miracles in your own life.

Begin today to realize that you live in an unlimited universe, with unlimited resources. There are billions of worlds in outer space and science is now beginning to realize that more worlds are being born every day. The secret power back of all creation is **intelligence.**

When you enter the domain of mind, nothing is impossible for you to achieve. You can create any kind of picture you wish to create within that inner world. You can release unlimited energy to build the outer world in the image and likeness of your innermost thought. There is unlimited life power flowing all about you, and all you need do to tap it is be aware of it, and give it a chance to express its dynamic power and intelligence through you. You need never be limited by circumstances in life; you need never be limited by lack of education, for even the most illiterate woman has the natural intelligence within her mind to create a perfect child. This universal mind works through your mind, and when you once learn how to direct it, and let your mind reflect its superior intuitive intelligence, you can achieve astounding things in your life.

How this Power Worked for Vince Edwards
(Ben Casey of TV)

One of the most striking examples of how this amazing power can work for a person and bring him from failure to one of the greatest successes of modern times in Hollywood, is that of Vincent Edwards, of Ben Casey fame in Television. Vince had been around Hollywood for ten years playing small parts, and a couple of featured parts in pictures that won little recognition. I had met him some years ago, and when I did a series of lectures in Hollywood in recent times, I urged him to come to some of my lectures on philosophy and psychology. The following week he came and showed great interest. He returned to several more, and then we had a private discussion one day about his personal problems relating to his career.

I told him, "You have power-potentials within your brain which you have not even yet begun to tap."

He grinned ruefully and said, "I've been trying to make a success in Hollywood now for ten years. I'm already a 'has-been' and I'm still in my early thirties."

Then I told him to use the methods given in this book, to visualize himself every day as being a big star in television and on the screen. I told him to go home that night and paste his name and photograph in copies of *Life, Look,* and *Saturday Evening Post,* visualizing these big national magazines giving him featured stories about his success. It sounded ridiculous, but Vince was willing to give anything a try. I also told him to write down on a piece of paper these words and to read them every night and morning, when he arose and when he went to bed, so they would imprint themselves upon his higher mind. "I will become a big star in the near future, and my life story will appear in *Life* magazine, *Look,* and *Saturday Evening Post.*"

Then to change his type and give his visual image of himself new impetus, I took about fifty photographs of him, showing a sympathetic type of personality, instead of the villain type that he had formerly portrayed.

These photographs he began to use to build his new career. He came to our lectures for several weeks, studied the laws and principles which we are learning in THE MILLION DOLLAR SECRET, and just a year later, Vince was selected from two hundred aspirants for the role of Ben Casey in the series that brought him fame and fortune. The astounding thing about it is that the very magazines Vince had written down, all carried big stories about him, and he became a nationally and even internationally famous person in a short time. Decca records paid him $250,000 for an album of his songs, and he is on his way to making the million-dollar fortune which he envisioned when he began his study of THE MILLION DOLLAR SECRET.

You can Call upon this Master Mind

You can call upon this Master Mind that is within you and ask it to bring you the money you want, the recognition in your work; the talents and gifts you desire; the home you want to own, the love-happiness in marriage you seek; all these things and more can be yours if you let this intuitive power flow through you and do not negate it by dwelling on thoughts of fear, worry, and hate.

Think big and you will be big! Think that you are inferior, unworthy of the good things of life, and you will instantly cancel out all the wonderful work that the Master Mind is trying to do for you.

The story is told of a circus manager who advertised a midget that could be seen in his sideshow for twenty-five cents. A lady went in, took one look at the so-called midget, and came out raging to the manager, "I paid a quarter to see the midget you advertised, but that gangling brute in there is no midget—he's at least five feet tall. I want my money back!"

The quick-witted manager replied, "But madam, that's the wonderful thing about this midget; he's the biggest midget in the world!"

Be the biggest and best of whatever you are. Have faith that the dynamic Master Mind that created you had in mind for you a unique and different destiny from any other person in the world. Use the Law of Adaptation that works in all nature, and adapt to the conditions of your life, using all your mental and physical resources to the best of your ability.

You may have been born short or tall, with features that are not too pleasing, but you can overcome even these physical shortcomings by calling on your higher mind to give you the necessary directions and intuitive guidance to find your right destiny. Martha Raye had a mouth considered too big by some; so did Joe E. Brown; both became great comedians. Schnozzle (Jimmy) Durante was told fame was impossible with his big nose, but he turned it into an asset instead of a liability. Garbo had feet considered by some much too big for grace, but she became one of our greatest stars. Beethoven was deaf, so was Edison; both overcame this defect and achieved greatness. Steinmetz was a hunchback; Lincoln was ugly and ungainly; Helen Keller became both deaf and blind; Milton was blind; Robert Louis Stevenson was sick most of his life—and yet all these people achieved outstanding success because they let this higher mind within them lead them on to fame and fortune.

Think Heroic Thoughts

Voltaire once said, "To be a hero, think heroic thoughts." To be great you must dwell in the company of great thoughts and high ideals. Your mind becomes stronger and more intelligent when you pass through it great thoughts, when you desire great things in your life, when you strive for high achievements. Mediocre success comes from holding mediocre thoughts. To expand your thinking into an area of importance and success, there must be a corresponding degree of inspiration and energy-drive in your thinking. If the idea held in consciousness is big enough, all the actions that follow will be of a like quality and degree.

It takes no more energy mentally to think of a big job, with good pay, than it does to think of an inferior position with small pay. People will set the value on you and your talents that you set on yourself.

The Man Who Conquered George Bernard Shaw

I once spent a delightful evening with a man named Gabriel Pascal. He had never been heard of before, but suddenly he became a famous name in Hollywood. He was the man who won George Bernard Shaw over to giving his plays for production in motion pictures. Pascal had no money, no reputation, but he had a tremendous idea—to see Shaw's great plays as movies.

Pascal hitch-hiked from London to Shaw's home in the country. He was so filled with enthusiasm that he was able to gain access to the great dramatist's home. In one hour of conversation he sold Shaw completely on his big idea, and Shaw signed an agreement then and there to let Gabriel Pascal produce his plays on the screen.

Pascal made a fortune through that contract, but what is more important, he brought to the world the greatness of Shaw, through the broad media of motion pictures that could reach millions of people.

What if this great producer had hesitated for a moment and thought himself too poor, too inadequate, to face the formidable

Shaw? He would instantly have doomed himself to failure. The
fact he listened to his inner, intuitive voice, when it told him he
was great and could achieve greatness, gave him the courage to
act with boldness and audacity. You can only conquer life when
you conquer yourself. Your mind must envision the big dream, the
high goal, and then you must turn to the power within your mind,
which we call the Million Dollar Secret, and let that power guide
you to the fulfillment of your destiny.

You can Change the Circumstances of Birth

Some people lose sight of their true inner greatness because they
are born in limited circumstances. Their families may have been
poor, socially unimportant, living in a part of town where there
was poverty and squalor. Should the true greatness of the human
mind and soul be restricted by such accidental circumstances of
birth? No, man should be able to triumph over such negative and
depressing circumstances in life. Such a man was Lincoln. It is
said that he failed nine times before he achieved any worthwhile
goal, and then it was a success that was so stupendous that he has
achieved imperishable fame. Hundreds of books have been written
on the life of Lincoln. His triumph over adversity and failure is
so monumental that it serves as an inspiration to millions.

Another instance where a great man was born in limited circumstances and overcame them to rise to great heights of achievement was that of George Washington Carver. I once visited this
noted black educator at Tuskegee Institute in Alabama, a few
years before he died. Carver was born to slave parents in the south.
He had to forge for himself early in life, educating himself and
breaking through the limiting barriers of race and color, as well
as environment. He achieved eminence as an educator, horticul-
turist and scientist because he had enlarged his concept of himself
and his mental powers. His mind was freed of the shackles that
enslave millions and he became one of the great men of his race
and country.

Dr. Carver showed me over three hundred products which his
higher mind had shown him how to create from the lowly peanut.
There were such products as varnishes, paints, insulating mate-
rials, fodder for cattle, fertilizers and oils. He never accepted the
limitations of his birth or the poverty-stricken environment in

which he was born. He changed the economy of the south because of his vision and daring.

Be the Genius You Believe You Are

There is great power in believing you are truly a genius. You must do more than believe however, you must BE!

Be successful by first acting and thinking success. You need not have a fortune to be successful. Many rich people are **not** successful in the real sense of the word. Riches do not designate true success. You can be successful as a person, and have great ideas, and gradually, recognition and monetary success will be yours. You must first cultivate the qualities of your mind which make for genius, before the world will reward you with its acclaim and fortune.

Let us see how another great man in the field of horticulture achieved greatness. His name was Luther Burbank. He believed in the power of the universal mind that creates all things. He looked at the products of nature and decided that he could improve in many ways, the things this universal mind created. It was a daring and even presumptuous concept that he brought to the world of horticulture. He had faith that he could, through cross-pollination, grafting, and selective planting, could produce better and more abundant crops. He worked to eliminate inferior brands of fruit and vegetables, and he produced bigger potatoes, seedless oranges and grapefruit, and many completely new varieties of fruits and vegetables through his experiments.

Change Your Mental Concepts and Change Your Life

If you begin today to change your mental concepts about yourself and your abilities, you will change your life radically. Stop being satisfied with your present limited salary and work. There is nothing wrong with wanting to better yourself. It is not wrong to want to make a great deal of money so you can give your children a better education and better conditions in life. You have a right to demand the best life has to offer. But you must really begin to believe you were born to inherit the earth and all therein.

All great men who have ever achieved anything worthwhile or

enduring, have been infused with this higher purpose in living. There must be a change in your mental concept first; the idea that you want to express, the work you want to do, the home you want to live in; when you once **know for sure** what it is you want, and you hold tenaciously to that idea, your circumstances of life will gradually begin to change. Do not worry about how this higher mind within you is going to produce the change. You cannot tell this infinite intelligence, which rules the world, how to create an oak tree; this is God's secret. But you can plant the tiny acorn in the soil and then, under the universal laws of growth and capillary attraction, that acorn will attract to itself all the nourishment it needs from the soil and rain, to make a giant oak tree a hundred feet tall.

How a Poor Minister Used this Million Dollar Secret

A minister named Frank Gunsaulus had a very poor church in the stockyard district of Chicago. He was imbued with a big dream; to bring higher education to poor people who could not afford to send their children to college. The higher mind dictated to him a title for a sermon he was to give. He advertised it in the newspapers the following Saturday. It was: "What I Would Do If I Had a Million Dollars."

That Sunday his church was packed with the curious, anxious to see what he was going to say. The minister was so fired with the fervor of his big dream that he spoke eloquently on the subject. At the end of the sermon a man who had been sitting in the front row, got to his feet and said, "I believe in your dream. I will give you a million dollar check on Monday, if you will call at my office. My name is Phillip D. Armour."

The Armour Institute of Technology was born in that moment. It has long been one of the most important schools for higher technological education in America.

Things to Do to Make You Greater

1. Keep your mind free of all discouraging thoughts such as failure, inferiority, poverty and inadequacy. Just as a magnet is magnetized by giving it metal to cling to, so too, your brain is magnetized to greatness by giving it big ideas to incorporate in

its convolutions. Think big thoughts; see big goals ahead; talk success, think of being great; visualize yourself doing unusual and successful things.

2. Build your sum total of knowledge. Knowledge is power. You will grow in mental power as your fund of knowledge grows. Study books that improve your mind. Try to make friends of people who are in important positions, or who are socially higher than yourself. You can often take on some of the luster of greatness by this association with greatness.

3. Learn to crawl before you walk, but try to run as quickly as you gain strength and confidence in your power to walk. In other words, do **not** stay in a position that is inferior or that does not pay you adequately. As soon as you have made adequate preparation for something better give up your inferior position and move briskly up the ladder of dreams to a higher goal. A muscle grows by use; brain cells evolve to greatness by using them.

4. Make decisions quickly. Do not vacillate after making a decision, but act on your decision promptly. Better to make a wrong decision than to freeze into positions of inertia and inferiority because you are not able to make a decision. Most of the great men and women who have done big things in history learned to make quick decisions and then act on them.

5. Write letters to important people presenting your great ideas. Some people have won promotion and success through this process of calling attention to themselves. Send night letters to persons you wish to interview for positions or to present your ideas. Everyone is impressed by a telegram. Great people do things in a lavish and different way from people who are mediocre and fearful.

6. Do not be afraid to ask important people to help you. They are human, and are often flattered to think that you believe they are important enough to give you assistance. Many great men have risen to positions of power through asking favors of those in big positions. Men like Carnegie, Schwab, Rockefeller, and even Lincoln knew this secret and used it.

You are greater than you think! Think and act like the great person you really are. People will respect you to the degree that you really believe you are great.

Self-Evaluation Chart

The following chart, if filled out honestly, will show you at a glance what value you set on yourself and your abilities. Remember—the world sets a value on you that is in keeping with your own idea of your true worth.

1. Are you working to perfect yourself at present?
2. Do you have a high estimate of your value?
3. Do you give full value to the job you hold?
4. If dissatisfied with your present job, are you making efforts to get into new work?
5. Are you taking any specialized courses in evening or correspondence schools to improve yourself?
6. Do you feel you are worth $25,000 a year salary?
7. Do you try to enlarge your contacts socially to meet important people who could help you advance?
8. Are you constantly thinking up new ideas to improve your work or your products?
9. Have you studied, or are you studying public speaking with a view to improving yourself for advancement?
10. Do you consider yourself a person of refinement and culture?

All questions in the above self-evaluation test should be answered "yes." Score yourself 10 points for each question. 70% indicates you should work more to improve yourself. 80% indicates you are making good strides forward. 90% indicates you are undoubtedly executive caliber. Less than 70% indicates you must still work very hard to raise your value of yourself and your talents.

4

Tap the Hidden Treasures
within Your Mind

A gold prospector once discovered a mine in the Nevada desert. He worked it feverishly for a few months, apparently exhausting its supply of gold after a few exploratory diggings. He had invested sixty thousand dollars in mining equipment and he was slowly going broke. When the mine petered out he became discouraged and sold his equipment and the mine to a junk man for a fraction of its original cost.

The junk man decided to continue digging where the other man had left off and two feet further he discovered a vein of gold that brought him a fortune. The gold mine continued to yield more of the precious metal until the junk man finally made a fortune of over five million dollars.

Two feet stood between the prospector and a fortune! If he had had the daring to continue for a while longer, he would have been well rewarded for all his effort.

There is a great deal of resemblance between your mind and a gold mine. Both contain hidden treasure. Just as you must dig the gold out that is in the mine, so too, you must explore and work to tap the hidden treasures that are hidden within your own mind.

What is the priceless ore that lies hidden within your mind? It is the golden substance of **ideas**. This is the only treasure that man truly possesses. Ideas have revolutionized the world. Ideas have built empires, created vast fortunes for men and women who started life with nothing. Your mind is an untapped source of treasure and you may begin today to explore this realm of ideas and find the pure gold of thought that will bring you a million dollar fortune. But there are other priceless golden nuggets within the human mind, that are worthy of discovery; the gold of happiness, friendship, love, companionship; the treasures of health and vitality, of talents and accomplishment. When you once learn how to tap the hidden treasures within your mind, you will discover a whole golden world of joy and beauty that you can share with others.

The Fabulous Firsts of Life

Every great fortune has been built from what I call the fabulous firsts. Someone has a new and original idea that has never been thought of before. This may be for a new design for a car, a new method of merchandising, new hair styles, new cosmetics, or a new corset design. These new fabulous firsts have the advantage of right timing and capture the public interest and imagination because of their daring concept.

We see these instances all around us of ordinary men and women who have tapped the priceless treasures of their minds through exploring the realm of ideas.

Charles Revson who founded the Revlon company had a big idea that he related to the field of cosmetics. He lived in the realm of beauty; he loved color. He studied different color schemes and asked himself: "Where does color look best?" He decided that it looked best on a woman. He set to work to create new and subtle shades of color in make-up; his shades of lipstick, finger nail polish and other fabulous products have built his business into a multi-million dollar a year bonanza. If Charles Revson had gone into any other field with his fabulous first ideas, whether it was merchandising, design, decorating, or manufacturing of some industrial product, he would have used the same priceless gift to achieve success. He dared to be different; he dared to release new and wonderful ideas from the treasure house of his mind and it brought him a fortune.

Another man tapped the treasure of his mind with an original idea. He is a dispenser of hot dogs in fabulous Coney Island. But he is not an ordinary man; he applied this same rule to the lowly hot dog, of being a fabulous first. He doesn't serve just ordinary hot dogs; he outsells all his competitors because he advertises that his hot dogs are a foot long!

A gas station owner in California did a very poor business, until he began offering a complete set of glasses with the purchase of ten gallons of gas or more. His business zoomed and soon he had three successful filling stations.

The birth of the trading stamp idea poured millions of dollars into someone's pocket, and changed the whole concept of modern merchandising.

One lady who operated a beauty parlor that was going broke, tapped the gold mine of her mind, and came up with an idea that added distinction and originality to her business. She took an ad in the local papers saying, "A Hollywood beauty expert will give every lady who comes into our shop a *free* beauty analysis and suggestions for the care of her hair and skin." The customers swarmed to the beauty salon for the free analysis. They didn't realize, of course, that the beauty expert was advising new treatments for the hair and skin which enormously raised the prices of the beauty treatments and soon tripled the income of the salon.

A tearoom did a very small luncheon business until they put out a sign in their window advertising, *Swami from India will give free crystal ball reading with lunch.* The price of the luncheon was raised to $2.50. The Swami received no salary, for he booked private readings at $5.00 each, for a half hour consultation after hours. The tea room was soon making more money than they ever dreamed of.

There Is Gold in Your Ideas

You may not think your ideas are valuable because they came from your brain. Change your attitude about the value of your thoughts. Some of the greatest things in the world were accomplished by men and women like yourself, who had just **one good idea** and made it pay huge dividends.

When I was lecturing in Honolulu recently, I met a man at my lectures who had invented the silent mercury switch for electric lights. He had been awakened so many times by the noise of the electric switch when his wife would turn it on at night, that his mind began to think of some way to make the turning on of a light switch, silent. He finally hit on the lucky idea of using a mercury switch which was completely noiseless. This one idea made him a fortune. While I was in Honolulu he put his private plane at my disposal to go see the Islands, and offered me the use of his private limousine and chauffeur to drive me anywhere I wished to go. A generous man, as well as a creative one.

Your ideas may be worth a fortune. You must sit quietly in your own room for at least half an hour a day and probe the gold mine of your mind. You should then write down all new ideas that come to you for improving your life, perfecting some product, marketing some merchandise you have created . . . for these ideas can be converted into real gold.

Start with whatever field you are in now, do not wait for some better time or more improved conditions. Look around you, see what could be changed or improved, and then set about doing it. Start this process now and continue it the rest of your life and you will see amazing results. Someone has said, "Practice yourself, for heaven's sake, in little things; and thence proceed to greater."

The man who invented the button hole made a fortune. The man who discovered the collar button made a million. Another man who was at a self-improvement type of lecture heard the speaker say, "Look in front of you, see your fortune there." The man took this statement literally and looked straight ahead. There was a lady with a large-brimmed hat directly in front of him. He started thinking, "My fortune is in that hat." He kept that idea in the forefront of his mind until finally, before he left that hall, an idea for a new type of hat pin came to his mind that later made him a fortune!

Value of Patience

So many people think of success in terms of making a million dollars; they seldom stop to realize that success is relative. You can be a success in your field here and now, in whatever situation you find yourself, if you will learn how to explore the gold within your mind. It is a process that takes a little time. Seldom does big success come over night. It is generally the accumulation of ideas that eventually form an overall pattern of greatness and achievement.

Epictetus said, "No great thing is created suddenly, any more than a bunch of grapes or a fig. If you tell me that you desire a fig,

I answer you that there must be time. Let it first blossom, then bear fruit, then ripen."

The idea you plant in consciousness will eventually grow and bear fruit, but you must give yourself time, and not be impatient and, like the gold prospector, give up just before you strike it rich.

Importance of Imagination

Some of the greatest things in life have been achieved through the creative power of the imagination. Everyone can use the power of imagination to build his future fortune. It takes only a little practice to develop this art of seeing the things in our mind's eye that we wish to create. There is some tremendous creative intelligence within your mind that expresses itself most powerfully when you use your imagination.

The life principle is inherent in the idea you hold in mind. This idea is like the seed you plant when you want a crop. It will produce wheat, corn, or thistles, depending on the nature of the seed. The creative imagination in man seems to be the fount of all life. Whatever seed or idea you hold in imagination seems to grow and evolve under the force of the Life Energy.

Imagination has created all the great inventions, products and artistic masterpieces in the entire world. When you see something like the Empire State Building, you are seeing the expression of an idea that was born in some man's creative imagination. The means to build it, the financing, the labor, all these things came naturally in the wake of the big idea that some man imagined—in this case the late Alfred E. Smith.

The industry of the entire south was changed through just one man's creative imagination. This man sat one evening watching his cat trying to pull his pet canary through the bars of his cage. But the cat only succeeded in getting a paw full of feathers, for the iron bars of the cage protected the canary. In his imagination this man visualized an iron claw pulling cotton off the seed, through iron bars. In that moment Eli Whitney's cotton gin was born. The creative imagination that could cause his mind to see this amazing invention changed the course of history of the south.

Kaiser and Imagination

During the second World War, the government desperately needed amphibious landing ships by the hundreds to land their troops on distant enemy shores. Every ship builder said it would be impossible to produce these ships quickly. But one man named Kaiser said he believed he could produce thousands of these ships on an assemblyline. His daring and vision were rewarded and the war was won quicker because of this man's amazing imagination. When I was in Hawaii I was amazed at the new projects Kaiser has undertaken, building a whole new area on the water front, which will be worth hundreds of millions of dollars. Kaiser uses the Million Dollar Secret we are studying in this book. Indeed, all great industrialists use it; all creative artists, writers, composers, use it. In Kaiser's case he has vision and daring, coupled with a terrific imagination. I have been told that he has had the word **impossible** cut out of his dictionary. He has implicit faith in himself and in his ideas. This is his Million Dollar Secret of success.

The Little Golden Nuggets in Your Back Yard

Some people look at the stupendous things achieved by great men, the enormous fortunes they have created, and they instantly say, "But I don't want the responsibility of making a million, or of building a big industrial empire. I want only enough money to give me and my family security and the better things of life."

What of the little golden nuggets that lie in your own back yard, then? If you are the type of person who does not wish to be saddled with too much responsibility, or too great a fortune, you can use these same secrets of creative mind for building a modest income and giving you and your family security for the future.

A man who worked in a cotton mill down south was such a man; he wanted security, but he made only twenty dollars a week and he was a long way from wealth. He tapped the hidden power of his creative mind, and began to think of some way to improve the business of weaving. His mind gave him a new idea for a new shuttle that he invented, and his financial problems were solved the rest of his life. The cotton mills have to pay him a royalty on every shuttle they buy.

Howard Hughes inherited some money from his father. He had enough to live securely for the rest of his life, but he was a creative man, who liked to accomplish things. He began to think of new ways to improve products having to do with oil well drilling and hit upon fabulous new ideas that made his small inheritance a fortune of hundreds of millions of dollars. One never knows where this creative gift will stop when you once start it going.

Another man decided to make malted milk shakes for a dime. Now he has over seventy thousand machines throughout the country, each person renting one, gives him a substantial amount for the use of his machines.

Daily Regime for Tapping Hidden Treasures of Your Mind

1. Begin each day, when you awaken in the morning, by passing through your mind a series of big ideas relating to your life, your work, your environment. Ask yourself: "What can I do today to improve my situation in life? How can I improve my business? What ideas can I incorporate in my work that will pay me rich dividends in the future?"

2. Check your mind and see if you are utilizing all the power that you possess or if you are wasting it on petty, unimportant things. Could you use more daring, courage, patience, persistence, thrift, sociability, optimism, humor, in your relations with others? Are you using the gifts and talents that you possess as stepping stones to greatness? Are you using the knowledge you possess fully? Do you seek the aid of the important people you've met, to help you achieve higher goals?

3. Look about you in your own work each day, and see what ideas you can think of that will help improve your product, or make more money for your company, or improve their product. One idea has made millions for some man. The man who invented nylon made a fortune. Frozen foods, shaving cream under pressure, the Diner's Club, magnetic tape, television, air conditioning, modern jet power, and Salk vaccine—all these were only ideas in some man's mind at first. They did something to bring their ideas into being.

4. Keep a daily diary in which you jot down each night the outstanding ideas you had during that day. Let your imagination soar without restraint, and carefully note the ideas and suggestions that flash into your mind. Then write them down for future use. Many times your subconscious mind will give you valuable ideas,

but if you do not write them down they leave suddenly and it is difficult to recall them again. Edison kept a notebook by his bedside, and his biggest ideas for his many inventions came to him while he slept. He wrote them down at once, and then the next day acted on these inspirational ideas.

5. Stir your mind to action by holding in your mind each day a desire to achieve something important and worthwhile. An artist cannot paint his picture until he first has the visual image in his mind. This desire to create that particular picture stirs him into action and he projects his mental picture onto the canvas before him. You must do the same thing; hold in your mind daily the pictures of the things you wish to achieve. Do not worry how you will attain them. The law of cause and effect takes over the moment you have a strong idea in mind, and leads you to take the steps that will bring fulfilment. Visualize yourself making more money; see yourself buying the things you desire; the new car, the house, the refrigerator, the fur coat; do not worry where the money will come from; hold the creative idea in mind that you *already have these things,* and soon you will be driven in the direction of achieving them.

Test Your Character

1. Do you feel that life has passed you by?
2. Do you think you are deserving of the better things in life?
3. Do you spend at least two hours a day on self-improvement?
4. Do you keep putting things off for the future?
5. Are you constantly cross and bad-tempered?
6. Are other people afraid of you?
7. Do you feel sorry for yourself?
8. Do you dread meeting people?
9. Are you constantly making negative statements?
10. Do you cry on other people's shoulders constantly?
11. Do you spend money carelessly? How?
12. Do you live in a disorderly, confused environment?
13. Do you neglect your appearance?
14. What worries you most in life?
15. Are you doing anything constructive to overcome your worries and fears?

16. Do you dissipate your creative energies?
17. Do you feel life has nothing to offer? Why?
18. Do you fear the future?
19. Do you try to get the best of everyone you meet?
20. Do you feel the world owes you a living?

Write down the answers to all the above questions; then read and study them over and over, and analyze your answers. There is no right or wrong answer, but you will know your own character better when you see how you answer the above.

5

Release Dynamic Energy
through Your Desires

Desire is man's prime driving force. Without this emotion man would still exist in a primitive state in caves and trees. Desire is the dynamic emotion that causes man to achieve greatness.

The human mind and body function at high levels of energy when the desires are activated in the right direction. If you use this positive emotion correctly it can release dynamic energy that will cause you to achieve anything you really sincerely desire. Ask yourself these questions:

Do you desire more money?
Are you anxious for a better job?
Do you want a new car? A new home? New furnishings?
Are you eager to go into your own business?
Do you desire love-fulfillment? Happiness in marriage?
Do you desire greater knowledge? More mental power?

These desires are natural and good. You should have them, in common with all humanity. If you do *not* have such desires, then you will never have the dynamic energy needed to achieve fulfilment in your life.

Let us study these desires and see how you may release hidden reserves of power within your mind and body, giving you the ability to achieve the things you desire.

The desire for food is what keeps the human body functioning.

The desire for money leads one to the acquisition of material treasures and objects. The desire for wisdom causes men to evolve their minds and become intellectual, and in turn, brings the race to new and higher realms of achievement. The desire for beauty causes artists to create masterpieces for the enjoyment of the world.

Strong Desires Give Great Achievement

If you desire something strongly enough you are already on the road to achieving it. Desire works its magic through the amazing power of the sympathetic nervous system. When you wish for something or desire it strongly enough, it becomes imprinted on your subconscious mind. The emotion is then transmitted to the nerves and muscles of your body, and you are impelled in the direction for achieving the things you desire.

If you desire more money, you will be gradually led to doing the things that bring you a fortune. If you desire friendship, you will act in such a way that others will be friendly towards you. Emerson said, "If you wish a friend, be a friend." The Law of Desire works unerringly to bring you that which you want. But there is a method by which you may implement your desires and set up actions and reactions in your mind, which will make it easier to achieve the things you desire.

Everyone thinks occasionally that he'd like to be rich, that he'd like to have a different personality, or change his work, or take a trip around the world; these are common desires of all humanity. But this type of thinking that is weak and casual is *not* the strong type of desire which brings fulfillment.

Your Blueprint of Destiny

To make your desires more positive and dynamic, I have discovered a method which I have used with success. I have given this Million Dollar Secret to thousands of my students, and they have also used it successfully to achieve seemingly impossible things in their lives. This same secret will work for you, if you use it and have implicit faith that it will work.

Write down your sincere, heart-felt desires on a sheet of paper. This helps bring them out from the depths of the subconscious mind into the light of reality. Head the sheet of paper as follows:

My Blueprint of Destiny: The Things I Desire in Life

Here is a sample list of some of the things people desire:

1. I desire more money to meet my needs. I would like to have the sum of one thousand dollars for immediate needs and the sum of fifty thousand dollars for an over-all goal in the future.
2. I want a business of my own. (State the type of business.)
3. I wish to change the nature of my work. I want to be a success as, (State here the type of work you prefer doing).
4. I desire my own home. (Describe the type of house you want, number of rooms, location, etc.)
5. I want a new car. (Make, color and style.)
6. I wish to create something artistic. (State whether you wish a creative gift like painting, writing, music, acting.)
7. I desire happiness in love and marriage and to find a suitable marriage partner with the following qualities. (Name these.)
8. I desire an electric refrigerator.
9. I desire a more magnetic and dynamic personality.
10. I wish to take a trip on vacation to Hawaii. (Or any other place you choose.)
11. I wish to meet important people socially and in business who will help me achieve success.

Then, on the bottom of this sheet of paper write these words. "I have faith that time is *not* law, and that I can achieve the things I have here written in a short space of time. I shall read this list over every morning when I arise, and every night, when I retire."

Then keep this Blueprint of Destiny somewhere where you can see it every day, and read it each morning and night. When you have achieved any of the things on the list, scratch them out and make out a new list. I even advocate that you completely re-write your list every week, thus refreshing your subconscious mind as to the things you desire.

How the Million Dollar Secret Worked for Me

Let me show you how this Million Dollar Secret worked its magic for me early in my career, when I discovered it. I was twenty-four years of age when I learned this priceless secret. I made out my Blueprint of Destiny, and, like most young people brought up in the age of the depression, material possessions meant a great deal to me. I put down on my list big and seemingly impossible things to achieve. I had faith that this power would work for me, and I dared ask for the biggest and best. To test this power I asked for some things that were seemingly impossible at that time of my life. It must be remembered that in the early thirties it was impossible to get a job and difficult to make money. I had no known resources, no parents to turn to for help, no influential friends. I had only my faith in the power within my mind to achieve the things that I desired.

I wrote down on my list, "I desire the sum of five thousand dollars cash, and one hundred thousand dollars as an over-all goal. I desire a beautiful home, a car, preferably the best, a Rolls Royce, and a career in writing." There were other things, smaller in scope, that I also listed. I read the list every morning and night, and re-wrote it in my own handwriting once a week. Within three months' time I made a contact with a group of magazines that contracted with me to do monthly articles for them. I began a large mail order business that soon began to pay off.

The five thousand dollars came in one lump sum from this business; I soon had ten people working for me, and one day driving down Sunset Boulevard, I saw a magnificent cream-colored Rolls-Royce for sale. It had belonged to the famous movie star, Gilda Gray. She had paid fifteen thousand dollars for it. I obtained it for seven hundred and fifty dollars cash. In the depression years no one could afford such a car, and yet, here I was, not only able to afford it, but having the audacity to believe my good fortune would continue indefinitely. And it did. I soon purchased a home for a small down payment. (This home later sold for one hundred thousand dollars, although I paid considerably less in 1935.)

In a short time I was meeting the most influential people in the motion picture industry: Louis B. Mayer, David O. Selznick, Irving Thalberg, Mervyn LeRoy, and such stars as Clark Gable, Gary Cooper, Norma Shearer, Marion Davies and hundreds of others.

Mary Pickford invited me to a party at Pickfair, where I met William Randolph Hearst, and Lord and Lady Mountbatten, H. G. Wells and many other world-famous celebrities. This was the beginning of the fulfillment of the desires I had written in my personal Blueprint of Destiny. As some of these things came true, I added others to my list, never once losing faith in the power that was manifesting these miracles for me.

Carnegie Hall and Bronze Plaques

If anyone had told me in my early years of struggle and poverty that I would one day become known as the Twentieth Century Philosopher of Carnegie Hall, I would have considered it a wild pipe dream. Later, when the owners of Carnegie Hall gave me two huge bronze plaques on the front of the hall announcing to the world that I was the Twentieth Century Philosopher, it was a dream come true. I knew then that I had discovered the Million Dollar Secret that lies within the mind, and which every person, no matter how limited his circumstances, may also tap and use.

One more illustration from my Hollywood cycle, which will help give you more faith in the Million Dollar Secret that can lead you to fame and fortune. A young Hollywood actor named Peter Lawford began attending some of our lectures with his mother, Lady Mae Lawford. He had hit a slump in his career and at that time he certainly never dreamed of the great destiny fate had in store for him. He and his mother practiced all these principles taught in this book. When Peter was young, Lady Lawford helped heal his arm through her faith and courage. The doctors wanted to amputate Peter's arm, which had been severely injured, but Lady Lawford trusted the higher intelligence which she knew was in her son's mind. The arm was saved and the doctors said it was truly a miracle of faith and prayer.

One night Peter Lawford came to my home in Bel Air to a party given for Lady Thelma Furness and Mrs. Gloria Vanderbilt. That night marked the turning point of his destiny. I introduced him to a charming young lady named Patricia Kennedy, whose brother, John F. Kennedy, was a Senator from Massachusetts. Three months later Peter and Pat were married. Peter Lawford found himself related to the President of the United States and was a frequent visitor to the White House. His career gained new impetus and he experienced a measure of success in his personal and professional life that he probably never dreamed possible.

The Million Dollar Secret works! It can work its miracles for you, if you have faith in this invisible power within your own mind and consult it about the moves you are to make in life. It will guide you as unerringly as it does the birds and animals, it will give you power to achieve your destiny as it does to the trees and flowers and crops in the field. Let us examine some of the ways by which this higher mind works for your good.

The Dynamic Life Urge

There is a dynamic force back of life which works in all nature. It is the Dynamic Life Urge. It gives you the will to live, the will to be, the will to create, the will to love. When you have a reason for living, this dynamic life urge becomes stronger and pushes you in the direction of your life goal.

Ask yourself this question: "For what do I live?" It must be for some purpose other than just making money, or eating, or a desire to have children. There must be a higher purpose back of your life than merely a desire to achieve fame and fortune. When you have a Master Motive to do good for others, to evolve the world, to discover something for the good of the entire world, then the Dynamic Life Urge flourishes and gives you energy and determination to achieve your goal.

Edison's Desire to Serve Humanity

What was Edison's motivating desire in life? Certainly it was not just to make money, although he lived to make millions of dollars through his numerous inventions. His life urge was to serve humanity, to give something of value to the world. This inner desire sparked his energy and made his mind so productive that he was able to create over three hundred inventions that have enriched the entire world. His phonograph, his movie camera, and his electric light bulb are only three of his many inventions.

Burbank had a Dynamic Life Urge that was completely unselfish and universal; a desire to benefit the world through the creation of his new products in vegetables, fruits and flowers. He released a constant flow of dynamic power from his higher mind that gave him inexhaustible energy and made him succeed so magnificently.

Albert Schweitzer, the noted physician and surgeon, worked in the jungles of Africa to heal the sick. Surely his Dynamic Life Urge is an altruistic one. He could make a fortune if he would open a clinic in some large city, but he prefers to help these unfortunate people who are far removed from the benefits of civilization. His reward? More than money can give; a deep, inner satisfaction that he is doing something great for the world.

Father Damien, the noted Catholic priest, worked with the lepers at Molokai, in the South Pacific, because their plight was so tragic and hopeless. He brought complete new techniques for the treatment of that dread disease, and sacrificed his life that others might live. Through his efforts, the modern treatment for this ancient scourge has removed most of the dread and danger of infection, and made the lot of the leper a much easier one.

The Light-Bringers of the Universe

Helen Keller and her work with the blind serves to illustrate magnificently how the Dynamic Life Urge can be released to help the unfortunate. The movie made around her life, *The Miracle Worker,* shows the heroic struggle that this great woman made to achieve her high place in history, as the light-bringer to the blind.

Jane Addams of Hull House in Chicago, was another example of how the Dynamic Life Urge can be channelized into creative work for those who are poor and underprivileged. Miss Addams turned her own home over to the poor children who had no one to care for them while their parents were at work. Although the doctors had given this frail, sickly woman only six more months to live, Jane Addams became so engrossed in her humanitarian work that she became strong and healthy and lived into her late eighties. She wrote in her autobiography, "I lived to bury four of the doctors who had pronounced my death sentence." Her life force was strengthened by her desire to help those who were unfortunate, poverty stricken and sick.

Beethoven and How He Released the Dynamic Life Urge

One sees very litle connection between the Dynamic Life Urge and the ability to compose great music, and yet, in the case of Beethoven, this great force found expression in his music through his unselfish acts in life. The story is told of how Beethoven was walking with a friend one cold, winter night, in a city in Germany where he was giving a concert the next night. Suddenly he heard someone trying to play his Sonata in F, and doing a very bad job of it. Then he heard a girl's voice cry out, "Oh, I cannot do justice to it. It's so beautiful!"

Feeling sorry for the girl, Beethoven knocked on the door of the house. A young man answered it and admitted him. A young lady sat at the piano and it was obvious to the great composer that she was blind. Without telling them who he was, Beethoven asked if he might play the composition for her. Instantly, as his fingers touched the keyboard, they both realized it was the master himself playing.

When Beethoven had finished, the girl begged him to play more. The composer looked up at the soft, silvery moonlight pouring through the window and said, "I shall compose a sonata to the moonlight." His fingers glided over the keyboard, and he played for a long time. When he had finished, Beethoven said, "I shall call this composition, *Moonlight Sonata*." Then Beethoven gave two tickets to the young couple for his concert the next evening and he hurried home and sat up the rest of the night writing down the notes for his new composition.

Many times, as in this instance from Beethoven's life, great inspiration and dynamic creative energy flow from a desire to do something good for another person. Part of our Million Dollar Secret is bound up in this Dynamic Life Urge, the desire to help your family, to educate your children, to serve the world, to evolve the standards of civilization a step higher, to bring peace and brotherhood to the entire world. Power flows abundantly to meet all your needs in the moment you use your gifts and talents unselfishly for the good of others. There is a universal law which sets to work for us immediately, when we put ourselves in tune with this higher mind that is in the universe. If we follow the laws of nature, all things work for our eventual good.

Marcus Aurelius said,

"All that is harmony for thee, O universe, is in harmony with
me as well. Nothing that comes at the right time for thee is
too early or too late for me. Everything is fruit to me that
thy seasons bring. O Nature. All things come of thee, have
their being in thee, and return to thee."

Do these Things to Release Dynamic Energy

1. Set some goal for yourself that you are trying to achieve.
Make that goal big enough so that it will excite your imagination
and arouse tremendous interest. Your energies will rise in proportion to the needs you have. If you have a goal to make only fifty
dollars a week, this is **not** a very inspiring goal. If you push that
goal and set a figure such as two hundred and fifty dollars a week,
instantly your subconscious mind will release the **dynamic energy**
and the **dynamic ideas** to make it possible to achieve the larger sum.

2. Have some person or persons in your life that you are trying
to help; this can be your own mate, your children, your mother
and father; whatever it is that you are trying to do for others
unselfishly will automatically give you greater energy and more
stamina to endure and persist. If you live just for yourself, it is
unlikely that you will have more than just enough life-force to
exist. Florence Nightingale was the first woman in history to go
out into battle to help nurse soldiers. She freed womankind from
the restrictions of their sex, and created a new and honorable profession for women. This frail woman was so inspired by her desire
to help the sick, that it gave her tremendous energy and vitality.

3. Find work that you really enjoy doing, and if you happen to
be in work you despise get out of it as soon as possible. Nothing
will so quickly lower the curve of energy as being in work you
detest. It has even been known to make some people chronically
sick because they are constantly frustrated. This restricts the
glandular action of the body and depresses the body organs. But
if you are in work you love, your body cells sing with joy and
health and energy, they are stimulated, so that you constantly feel
good.

4. Have hobbies that give you pleasure as well as relaxation.
Dynamic energy is created when your mind is interested in doing
something. It is vitally important that you have avocations as well
as a vocation. The moments you give to painting, writing poetry

or stories, modelling in clay, stamp collecting, rug weaving or whatever hobby you indulge, are moments well spent, for they will serve to release energy which will make your regular work easier and less boring.

5. If you are not already in love with someone, fall in love as quickly as you can. Nothing helps release dynamic energy so quickly and potently as being in love. Science is now aware of the importance of this powerful emotion in our lives. Children thrive and are healthy when loved. When denied love they are sickly and lacking in energy and interest. Later, we shall learn more about this powerful emotion, for it is one of the big and important revelations of our Million Dollar Secret.

6. Set daily goals for yourself that you are trying to achieve. If you are a salesman, set a certain number of sales. If an author, set a certain number of pages you wish to write. If a student, a certain course of study which you do regularly. It has been found that the mind responds to the challenge of direct suggestion. If you know you are going to play eighteen holes of golf, the body and brain see to it that the necessary energy and drive are created to carry you through that course. If a prize fighter builds himself up mentally to take on a certain opponent, his body will release the energy to carry him into that ring facing formidable opposition. As you achieve these small goals at first, keep raising the level of your goal, until you have reached a high peak of energy and achievement.

7. Each day, when you start your activities, say a series of suggestions that will be energy-boosters to your subconscious mind. Here are a few you might memorize and repeat every day when you feel the need of inspiration or greater mental or physical energy.

"I am strong and healthy. I can accomplish anything I desire."

"I am young and vital, and my body now responds with new energy and vitality to do all my tasks today."

"I am happy, happy, happy. I find joy in my work and my life sparkles with interest and happiness."

"I have faith in myself, my work and my destiny. I now extend this faith to the entire world."

"I am successful, well-liked, and attract friends to myself. I now radiate confidence, poise and inner power."

"I love everyone I meet, and they will in turn love me."

"I am rich as any millionaire; with the gifts of mental and

physical health, free estates of parks, and the golden gifts of friendship, love, peace, happiness and beauty."

Whenever you feel tired or discouraged, or your energy is low, just stop whatever you are doing, breathe deeply for ten or fifteen times, say all of the above energy-boosters, and really mean them, then you will see how quickly your mind recovers its sharpness, and your body becomes filled with new energy and vitality.

Are You an Efficient Personality?

1. Do you jump right up in the morning when you awaken?
2. Do you organize your life, your work, your play?
3. Do you tackle unpleasant tasks rather than put them off?
4. Do you keep your financial records straight?
5. Is your environment as neat and orderly as possible?
6. Do you make out lists of things you want to do?
7. Do you live your life according to a time schedule?
8. Do you have a budget that you adhere to?
9. Do you sit down and think about your life at least an hour a day?
10. Do you have a good memory?

The answers to all the above questions should be *Yes*. This would indicate that you function on a very high plane of efficiency. However, most people cannot achieve this high degree of efficiency overnight. If you answer less than seven of the above questions Yes, then you need to work to build your mental efficiency.

Rate yourself 10 points for each Yes answer. Seventy or more indicates fair efficiency; 80 is excellent, 90 is better than most, and 100 means you have achieved great efficiency.

Twenty Barriers You Must Overcome to Achieve Fortune

1. Procrastination; putting things off until a better time.
2. Fear of failure.
3. Indecision, not knowing what you want or where you are going in life.
4. Confusion, chaos and disorder in your personal life.
5. Extravagance and waste with your money, time and energy.

6. Putting yourself in positions of failure, and inferiority.
7. Being afraid of big goals, important people and big money.
8. Vacillation, going from one thing to another, without knowing what you really want in life.
9. Living under concepts of limitation financially and otherwise.
10. Lack of faith in yourself, your talents, your future.
11. Lack of intense desire to succeed.
12. Building negative habit patterns of worry, fear, hate, jealousy, envy, and other negative emotions that short-circuit the power-house of your brain.
13. Failing to recognize an opportunity when it is presented.
14. Being afraid to take chances in life.
15. Failing to use your imagination.
16. Not dreaming or thinking big enough.
17. A personality that is inferior, inadequate and self-conscious.
18. Ignorance, due to lack of education.
19. Fear of trying new things because they are unfamiliar.
20. Not understanding money and how to use it creatively.

6

Magnetism, the Law of
Universal Attraction

What power is it that causes some men to attract a million dollar fortune, while others remain poor and in want all their lives? If you once could discover the answer to that question you would know the secret in back of making a fortune. I believe that I have discovered just such an answer, and it is a big part of our Million Dollar Secret that lies within your mind. The great and universal Law of Magnetism is the secret power that is back of **all life**. Science now believes that magnetism and electricity are an indivisible unit, that they produce all living intelligence and motivate all life. This power of magnetism is the energy, the life force that exists between all atoms and gives them their cohesive unity.

Take the planets spinning in space for instance; they are held in their orbits by gravity, which is another name for magnetism. When Newton discovered the law of gravity, he laid the foundation for our modern jet planes and space ships. Magnetism, too, is **a** reality.

How Magnetism Gives You Power to Attract

Magnetism can be physical and material, as between objects and things; it can also be mental. The mind that sets up a magnetic attraction to the things that it pictures and concentrates on, has the power to attract those things to itself. This accounts for the tremendous magnetic attraction that misers have for money. They concentrate on nothing but getting and hoarding money. This becomes their obsession; day and night they think of money. Their minds become just like magnets; they live and think and breathe money. They deny themselves everything so they may save more money. They gradually build a fortune, but it does them no good, for they have used this magnetic law negatively. Just think if you learn how to use this magnetic law in a positive manner, what amazing things you could do with it.

How does magnetism work to attract to you the things you want? Take an example in physics; a piece of iron is wrapped with copper wire and electric current is passed through it. The bar of iron becomes a magnet, and can attract to itself any metal that has the same molecular structure or vibration as itself. You have seen enormous cranes with a big magnetic ball attached, picking up tons of scrap metal. This is the principle of the magnet.

Now visualize your mind filled with magnetic thoughts of success, money, friendship, love, health, happiness, things you want to own. The mind becomes literally magnetized by these thoughts, and the electric current flows from the brain to the nerves and muscles of your body, the sympathetic nervous system, which is a part of the automatic nervous system, reacts automatically; it follows the instructions of your conscious and subconscious mind implicitly. The instructions go out, as by a wireless message, "Bring me more money. Make me a success. Give me great ideas. Lead me to people who can make me successful and help me. Find the hidden gold mine or oil field. Give me great gifts and talents."

As you magnetize your mind more and more with these or similar thoughts you gradually become a magnet, mentally and physically, able to attract to yourself the conditions and things you have put into your mind.

The Secret of Mental Imagery

When you picture something as coming true for you, the very act of picturing or mental imagery, sets into motion the forces that will attract it to you.

I know a man who was in the South Pacific, and he cut a picture of Ruth Hussey, the movie actress, out of a magazine. She represented his ideal for love and marriage. He carried that photo with him, looked at it at night before going to bed, mentally imaged himself married to her. Months later, he was at a big party in San Francisco, and he looked up and saw a girl dressed in white walking towards him, as though magnetized by him. He recognized her instantly; "The girl of my dreams!" he thought, with a thrill of excitement. They gravitated towards each other, drawn by the law of magnetism. They fell in love with each other, and were married. Who knows what strange powers man may tap when he enters this fourth-dimensional world of the mind and soul?

Dr. Rhine, of Duke University, has done research on these strange subjects, like extra-sensory perception, and he believes that science is on the verge of breaking through new frontiers of power in the discovery of a whole new world of mind and spirit. Einstein, at the time of his death, was working on a Cosmic Theory which would explain many of the things that are in the realm of the mind, and which often baffle people.

The secret of mental imagery consists in picturing the persons, conditions, money, success, objects—whatever it is that you want for your very own, and picturing them so strongly that they begin to live for you in the **realm of mind.**

The Bible speaks of this Law of Imagery in these words: "Let us make man in our image. . . ." This image can only be held in one place; in the mind, specifically in man's imagination. The very beginning of the act of creation is this ability to picture or image the things you want in your life.

The secret of all creation is locked up in the genes of the human body. This is its **image.** Children follow this pattern universally. The image is there in the life germ or cell that begins all life; two arms and legs; hair and eyes, and a nose and mouth; the picture pattern for the formation of the involved kidneys, lungs, heart, nerves and muscles. Even the coloration of the hair and eyes. What a miracle of creative genius that all these things should be contained in a cell so microscopically tiny that only the electronic microscope recently revealed nature's hidden secret for creating life.

What Is the Pattern in Your Mind?

The pattern you hold in your mind is analogous to this secret of the body's genes. In that invisible pattern of your brain there are electrical and magnetic forces that have power to radiate through your body, motivating you to create the destiny pictured in your mind.

This mental pattern works, for you can put into it persons you want to meet, things you want to do, money you wish to attract, things you wish to own—and, by some strange law of mental magnetism, which we know exists, although science does not yet know why it works—you may attract into your orbit of experience the things you image perfectly.

I remember two graphic examples of how I used mental imagery before I even knew about these mental laws of magnetism. I had always admired Mary Pickford in my early days. I suppose, like millions of others, I fell in love with America's Sweetheart, as she was known then. I dreamed of one day meeting her; I pictured this so strongly that it seemed to me I had already met her.

One day I was at a photographer's shop in Hollywood, where pictures had just been taken to illustrate a story I had written, when suddenly, framed in the doorway, stood Mary Pickford. The golden curls, the blue costume she wore for *Coquette,* the way I had visualized her in my dreams. We met, and through Miss Pickford, I was introduced to Hollywood, where my real career began.

Thoughts have repercussions. I had also pictured one day meeting William Randolph Hearst, and visualized that he would help me further my writing career. This thought was so magnetized that one night at a big party at Pickfair, Miss Pickford introduced me to the noted publisher. As in a dream, I talked to this great man for nearly an hour. Later he gave me the front pages of the *American Weekly* for a series of articles and illustrations, advertising a new book I had written, which sold thousands of copies. The front page of the *American Weekly* had never before been given to an individual, and Mr. Hearst did not give me one week's cover **but four!**

How can one doubt the magnetic power of mental imagery in the face of such evidence? This is only one illustration from my life, I have had literally hundreds of such miracles in my lifetime, and I can testify to thousands in the lives of my students over the years.

Another illustration to show the magnetic power of thought. Two members of our lecture group visualized winning the Irish Sweepstakes, one on the West Coast, the other in New York. In both cases these ladies won over one hundred thousand dollars!

Why doesn't everyone win the Irish Sweepstakes who visualizes himself winning? This is one of the mysteries of magnetism; some people use it more powerfully than others, or some people have *no other way* to magnetize money, and they become almost desperate in their desires, attracting it through such means. Others magnetize a fortune through going into business, inventing something, or writing a great novel. The power works differently for different people.

$25,000 Magnetized through a Song

Another instance of how this law of magnetism worked for a member of our lecture group, was that of a young man named Ted Mossman, who played the piano at some of our lectures in New York City, and who worked part time in a health food store. When he learned of this great Law of Magnetic Attraction he began to visualize himself making a fortune through writing songs.

A year later he came to me with a check for his royalties for twenty-five thousand dollars. The song was: *'Till the End of Time*. Through that song Ted went to Hollywood under contract to a big studio, and his success was assured.

Magnetize What You Want

You can magnetize what you want in life. You must image it mentally; clearly and emotionally, feeling it is already yours. You must write it down, as we stated in another part of this book. You must visualize the persons, conditions, money, success—whatever it is you want clearly and as often as possible. The process known as day-dreaming is helpful in fixing the image clearly in your mind. Day-dream yourself in the situations in life you desire; such as singing or speaking or acting on a stage. Do the entire performance, as if you actually were before that audience. Picture yourself in the job you desire, seeing yourself as an executive, giving orders, having other employees under you. Visualize yourself going to the bank and depositing checks or cash; or drawing the money out and going into shops and spending it. Spend time in looking at pictures of cars, fur coats, or houses and furnishings, in magazines and newspapers, and visualizing them as being in your possession. Cut these pictures out and paste them in a Scrapbook of Destiny, and look at these pictures every day, imagining them as being already yours.

Go window shopping, and stand before windows, fixing the mental images in your mind of jewelry, clothes, television sets, radios, hi-fi sets, whatever you desire, and then pass these mental images through your mind over and over, especially as you go to sleep at night; let these mental images be the last thing you pass through your mind.

A girl coming to our lectures did this act with a fur coat, specifically a mink coat. She was a maid in a home, and had *no way to buy* such a mink coat. She kept picturing it, and her mental imagery was so great that she magnetized a mink coat in one month's time. A rich woman in our lecture group bought herself a new mink coat. She had observed this other woman in her shabby cloth coat, and, without knowing a thing about her mental imagery, brought her old mink coat to class one night, wrapped up in a box, and gave it to the poorer woman. This amazing demonstration was brought to my attention. What magnetic power had caused this woman to actually attract a three thousand dollar mink, that was in wonderful condition? It was the Million Dollar Secret which we are discussing in this book. It works! It can work its magic for you if you use these principles and have faith in them.

How Magnetism Built Big Fortunes

If you wish to magnetize more money, you can do so through this method. Let it become a dominating desire in your mind. Remember, however, not to let your desire for money unbalance you, as in the case of misers. The Bible does *not* say to hate money, or that it is evil to have money; it only says, "The *love* of money is the root of all evil." But in the Bible it also says in Genesis 1:31, "And God saw everything that he had made, and, behold, it was very good." What is good, cannot be evil. It is good for you to have money, the things you need; you can do good things with money.

The desire to have a fortune will help magnetize money for you, but you must use money constructively, for the good of others. I once knew a woman who magnetized a fortune of eight million dollars, but when her husband died and she inherited it, she began to drink and gamble and spend her money foolishly. Soon she lost her fortune, her two million dollar home was sold for ten cents on the dollar, and she finally became so depressed that she committed suicide. She had used her money for evil and it destroyed her.

The great fortunes built by such men as Rockefeller, Carnegie, Vanderbilt and Astor, were not used for selfish purposes alone. They have given to the world great benefits. Carnegie magnetized hundreds of millions of dollars in his lifetime. He endowed twelve hundred libraries in his lifetime, and spent most of his fortune before he died, doing good for the world. He said that in the future it would be considered sinful for a rich man to die rich.

The Rockefeller millions are still benefiting the world, long after the death of the senior Rockefeller, who magnetized one of the greatest fortunes in the world. The Rockefeller Foundation was established, where scientific and medical research is going on continuously that may one day save your life or that of a loved one.

Henry Ford magnetized millions by his desire to give the world reasonable transportation. This unselfish dream was so magnetic that it attracted the fortune he built.

Mental Energy and Matter Interchangeable

Einstein proved that mental energy and matter are interchangeable. In other words, the energy of the mind can be converted into material substance with ease. For instance, the idea to build a bridge is only mental energy, but it can become externalized easily in the building of the actual bridge. The idea for a painting, a literary work, an invention, or a business, is just as real and has a dimension that is as solid and real as matter. The *idea for a thing* has inherent in it the ability to **magnetize** the thing itself and bring it into being. This is the way that your mental energy has in itself the equivalent for the thing you are holding in your mind. Be sure then that you magnetize *only* the good and positive things. If you use this law of magnetic attraction to picture accidents, sickness, failure and disaster, it will externalize these negative things for you. The law works to produce thistles or wheat, under the law of the harvest. The Bible speaks of it as, "As ye sow, so shall ye reap." This is the great law of magnetic attraction at work in nature. Sow an acorn and produce an oak tree; sow wheat and you have a crop of wheat. Sow thistles and only thistles can come forth from the same ground that produced the wheat or oak tree.

This is why some people, with the same brain cells, the same bodies, are able to produce only unhappiness, sickness, poverty and failure, from the same life-substance that others use to magnetize and produce health, happiness, fame, fortune and prosperity.

Take these Six Steps for Greater Magnetic Power

1. Picture clearly the things that you want to magnetize and attract. Sit quietly in your room and run these pictures through your mind like film through a movie projector. Review these pictures daily, as often as possible, especially at night just before going to sleep. See them clearly; do *not* keep changing them, but have the pictures the same each time. Have as many things as you want to magnetize, taking them up one at a time, and giving about ten minutes to picturing each thought.

2. Write down the things you wish to magnetize and attract. Write them clearly and briefly, as you have learned in another part of this book. This serves to imprint them upon your subconscious mind more forcibly.

3. Indulge in day-dreaming when possible to do so. The moments you spend waiting for a car or bus, the time you take out for coffee or a cigarette at your work—use these precious moments to day-dream. In these day-dreams see yourself in the work you want to do; living in your dream house; married to the mate who fits your needs; having money to do the things you wish; ideas and inventions that could make you a fortune.

4. *Do not tell anyone* of the secret power you are using. They will tend to laugh at you, to discourage you, and they may short-circuit your magnetic attraction with their negative ideas. Many a genius has never won recognition because he shared his dreams and secrets with friends or members of his family. The acorn grows in the secret, hidden womb of earth, safe from all interference, and becomes an oak tree because of this secrecy. What if someone tore it up by the roots every few days to see if it was growing? It would die. So too, your dreams die if they are shattered by others.

5. Have faith in the invisible intelligence that resides in nature, to produce the things you are trying to magnetize. The secret power that can make a baby in nine months' time, knows how to release the energy to bring your idea or dream to fruition. But you must have faith in this invisible power that creates all life. The chicken in the egg is evidence of this great miracle-working

intelligence. From that invisible cell it produces the feathers, beak, heart, lungs, and eyes of that chick. You can trust such an intelligence with your life.

6. Share your good with the world. There is magnetism in giving to others. The soil gives of its substance to the plant and enriches the world; the sun gives of its warmth and the world lives in its golden glow. All great givers have been able to attract more of this world's goods than the misers, for misers magnetize money but lose their lives by not sharing it with others. A shabby old woman was found dying on the streets of New York in midwinter. When a search was made of her shabby apartment a trunk was found that had five hundred thousand dollars in cash hidden in it. And yet, she died of starvation! The Bible states this law of magnetism through giving:

> Give, and it shall be given unto you. Good measure, pressed down and running over shall be given into your bosom. For with what measure you mete withal, it shall be measured unto you again.

7

The Magic Genie
within Your Subconscious Mind

In Aladdin's Lamp, the fairy tale tells us, re-
sided a Magic Genie, who would carry out any wish Aladdin had.
All he had to do was rub the magic lamp and the Genie would
appear ready to carry out his bidding.

Your subconscious mind might be likened to this Genie. It is
ready to carry out any command that you give it. And like the
Magic Genie, your subconscious mind is a powerful aid, a dynamic
force that can be harnessed for great achievement.

The Power of Your Subconscious

What is the subconscious mind? It is that part of your brain
which takes over all the automatic functions of the brain and
body. Here are some of its functions:

It builds the child's body in the mother's womb.
It repairs the body, if it is sick or injured.
It regulates the circulation of the blood, the blood pressure.
It controls the process of metabolism and digestion.
It regulates the heart beat and keeps it going when you sleep
  or are unconscious.
It regulates the glands of the body.
It controls the lungs causing you to breathe constantly.
It motivates the nerves and muscles of the entire body.

It rules the memory, visualization, imagination, the storing of millions of facts in the brain.

It controls the eyes, the contraction and expansion of the pupil of the eye.

It controls the five senses: sight, touch, smell, hearing, and feeling.

These are only a few of the functions of the subconscious. It is now believed by science to have many more useful functions which relate to health, happiness, success and well-being. Certain it is that your subconscious mind is the most potent force within your brain, which you may harness for great achievement.

The Miracle Worker within

Scientists now announce that the subconscious mind is more clever and resourceful than the conscious mind. It is the intelligence within the body that fights the germs that enter the blood stream, and which might cause blood poisoning. It is the power that knows how to coagulate the blood to stop bleeding, and which can weave new skin, when we are injured. Science has no idea how the subconscious accomplishes this miracle, but it knows how to keep the body healthy, or to heal it perfectly, if man should become sick.

It is in the subconscious mind that all the centers of automatic control for the body reside. It controls your heartbeat, the circulation of the blood, the regulation of the glands, the repair and building of the body. In addition to these automatic functions, it also regulates the habits of your body. You can train this subconscious, by building positive habits, to perform any act you choose consciously. When you see a great pianist like Horowitz sit at the piano and play a difficult concerto with such ease and fluency, it is because he has spent years in building the habit patterns of perfection in his mind. The subconscious mind stores these memories and releases them under automatic control, so the pianist need not consciously think of how he is going to play the difficult music.

All your habit patterns can be built in your subconscious mind so they become automatic responses of your body functions. You can learn how to become a great speaker, writer, composer, musician, inventor or business success. You may consciously choose the things you want your subconscious mind to do for you automatically, and then by constant repetition of the act or thought, you will imprint it on your subconscious mind, making it a part of the automatic reflex action of your subconscious mind.

Modern psychosomatic medicine has shown that one's mental attitude also has much to do with sickness or health. When you constantly repeat positive statements such as, "I am healthy, I am happy, I am young, I have vitality and energy," you actually help raise the energy-levels of your body and release the stored sugar in the liver, giving you greater vitality and improving your health.

On the other hand, negative suggestions, such as, "I am sick, I feel terrible, I am poor, I am old and friendless, I am tired, I will catch cold, I'm afraid I'll have an accident," actually create the mental and physical atmosphere in which these negative conditions will breed. It is the subconscious mind that elevates all your words and thoughts to the automatic realm of action, through the sympathetic nervous system. It is vitally important, then, that you constantly think, speak and write only positive words which you want your subconscious mind to externalize in your body as good health, and in your outer environment as order, efficiency, and success.

You can see what a tremendous force the subconscious mind is. It is part of our Million Dollar Secret for achieving success, health, happiness, prosperity, fame and fortune. When you once learn how to relegate most of the acts of your life to this Magic Genie within your brain, you will be free of mistakes, you will be able to make intelligent decisions, you will have intuitive power to guide you to the right situations in life. You will implement your present mental power, and increase your abilities a hundred fold!

Warren Hilton, in "Applied Psychology" wrote,

Considered from the standpoint of its activities, the subconscious is that department of mind, which on the one hand directs the vital operations of the body, and on the other conserves, subject to the call of interest and attention, all ideas and complexes not at the moment active in consciousness.

Observe, then, the possibility that lies before you. On the one hand, if you can control your mind in its subconscious activities, you can regulate the operation of your bodily functions, and can thus assure yourself of bodily efficiency and free yourself of functional disease. On the other hand, if you can determine just what ideas shall be brought forth from sub-consciousness into consciousness, you can thus select the ma-terials out of which will be woven your conscious judgments, your decisions and your emotional attitudes.

To achieve control of your mind is, then, to attain (a) health, (b) success, and (c) happiness.

How to Harness Power of Your Subconscious

Repeat the idea you want to imprint on your subconscious.

The subconscious mind accepts as truth whatever you tell it often enough. When you repeat an idea over and over again, your subconscious mind automatically accepts it as gospel and sets to work making it a reality in your life. In psychology, this is known as the Law of Predominant Mental Impression. It simply means that you must keep repeating an idea, saying it over so often that it becomes a law for your subconscious mind.

For instance, if you keep telling yourself, "I can't do that, I'm afraid I'll fail, I'm inferior and inadequate, I'm tired and weak, I'm afraid I'll catch cold," you will make these negative statements the laws of your subconscious mind. As this mind auto-matically carries out everything you think or say many times, the sympathetic nervous system will set these negative forces into mo-tion. You will become more and more fearful. You will do things that make you fail. You will become inferior. You will be con-stantly tired and weak, and catch cold often. You set the mental stage for the action you imprint upon your subconscious mind.

Change this negative repetition to a positive one. Say over and over to yourself or out loud, "I can do anything I wish to do. I am a success. I desire fame and fortune. I believe in my abilities to achieve greatness. I can make friends. I am loved by others. I can win a promotion and a raise in salary. I can sell merchandise to anyone."

When you repeat these and other similar statements to yourself hundreds of times, and keep this up the rest of your life, you are working with the Law of Predominant Mental Impression. Your subconscious will *believe* what you tell it and carry the commands you give it into action, producing the conditions in your body, and in your external world that you tell it to produce.

The Art of Impersonation

One of the best ways to reach your subconscious mind and imprint upon it the things you want it to do, is to begin to act the part you wish to play in life. If you want to be rich and successful, act as though you already are. If you want to be happy, begin to act as though you are already happy; smile, be optimistic, talk about the good things of life instead of the sad and evil things. Your subconscious reacts according to the emotional pattern that you set for yourself. If you act happy and successful, your subconscious will send positive pulsations to your glands and the entire rhythm of your body will change to a positive one.

When Napoleon decided he would become Emperor of France, he called in Talma, the leading tragedian of France to show him how to walk, talk and look like an emperor. Napoleon had a real problem, for he was scarcely five feet tall. The actor made him strut back and forth, giving commands as an emperor would, he showed him how to stand, how to talk, how to think like an emperor. Finally when Napoleon was ready to declare himself Emperor Napoleon the First, he carried such conviction that the crowned heads of Europe bowed before him!

If you act a part long enough, your subconscious mind will be impressed by it, and make it a living reality. You can begin to achieve a stronger, more dynamic personality by this art of impersonation. Stand before a mirror and speak to yourself. Tell yourself that you are strong, dynamic, good-looking; really believe the things you are going to become. Then go around *being* the person you wish to be. Soon, it will become second nature. You will be guided to doing the things you have long acted out. People will begin to see you as the person you have mentally thought yourself to be.

A Priest Who Thought Himself into Becoming a Bishop

A true story from life will illustrate this ability of the subconscious mind to create from the things you think and do, is that of a priest, who went around constantly thinking and acting as if he already were a bishop. The other priests talked about how he put on airs, and they were actually just a little jealous of him.

One day a bishop died, and another was being chosen by the

heads of the church to take his place. Who do you think they selected? The priest who already believed he was a bishop!

Reach Your Subconscious by Writing It down

Elsewhere we have told of the importance of writing down your desires and ambitions. Now it is time for you to know how this simple act works to imprint upon your subconscious mind the suggestions that you write down.

Your subconscious mind believes everything that is repeated to it often enough; things that are said or written down. The kinetic action of *doing* something with your hands more forcibly impresses the subconscious mind than if you just *think* a thing. You no doubt recall how the school teacher used to make children write something down on a blackboard hundreds of times as a form of punishment. We tend to remember that which we write down; the subconscious mind catches up the written instructions or demands, and incorporates the information in the automatic structure of the brain, already making it a reality.

One of the best methods for improving your memory is through imprinting things that you want to remember upon your subconscious mind. Writing it down several times will tend to fix it in your memory so that recall will be easier.

How Admiral Richard E. Byrd Used the Subconscious

When Admiral Byrd was only twelve years of age he was impressed by the fact that Admiral Peary had discovered the North Pole. He had a secret desire to become a great explorer. He wrote in his diary, "I shall be the first man to discover the South Pole." He forgot all about this inscription in his diary, but his subconscious didn't. It motivated his entire life, causing him to study navigation, mathematics, exploration, and all related subjects. Years later he actually did discover the South Pole!

Subconscious Power through Reading Aloud

One of the greatest secrets for releasing subconscious power in your personality is to read or talk out loud. There is something magical about the hypnotic power of the human mind. When you give yourself auto-suggestions, and believe what you are telling yourself, you are deeply imprinting the subconscious mind with what you say. If you will read positive, beautiful statements aloud, your entire personality will soon take on the coloration of the thoughts you are expressing. It is excellent training for your voice, your personality, your cultural growth, if you read the works of Shakespeare aloud, and even memorize some of his greatest soliloquies. It will give your subconscious mind a new impetus in the direction of magnetism, power, expression and beauty.

Winston Churchill was a modern genius who had developed his subconscious mind to an astonishing degree. Not only was Sir Winston a great statesman and a brilliant speaker, but he was proficient in writing, painting, and many other gifts and talents. He wrote his speeches down and spent a great deal of time polishing his words and style. In that way he achieved the exact shade of meaning he wanted. He used his subconscious mind fully, and that is why he had such an amazing career that spanned over half a century, and played such a dynamic role in world history.

Importance of Keeping a Diary

It is a good daily habit to keep a diary. In it you can jot down your ideas, as well as your dreams and aspirations. There is no doubt but what your subconscious mind is alert to everything you put into that diary, and you form habits of thinking that are neat, orderly and efficient.

Queen Victoria kept a diary throughout her entire life. No matter how arduous her day had been or how tired she was at night, she jotted down her main thoughts and activities for the day before retiring. It gave her mind the ability to make quick and important decisions and added a dynamic power of concentration when big events demanded her instant attention.

Review these Facts for Greater Subconscious Power

1. Turn over the automatic function of your body completely to your subconscious mind. Stop worrying about the way your body works and trust your subconscious to take care of it. Stop telling yourself that you are sick, old, tired, fearful. Begin to tell

yourself you are strong, healthy, powerful, young, that you have inexhaustible energy and vitality.

2. Use the system of auto-suggestion advocated by Coue, and every night when you get ready to go to sleep say over to yourself or aloud, at least twenty times, "Every day in every way, I am getting better and better."

3. Memorize other auto-suggestions which you repeat every day when you have a few moments time, such as: "I can do this job perfectly. I will win promotion and a raise in salary. I like other people and they will like me. I can be a big success. I will become rich. I am bigger than I think. I can do anything anyone else can do." You can make up your own suggestions to fit your needs. If you want to write a novel, give yourself suggestions that give confidence to your subconscious mind, such as: "I know I can write a great novel. I have great ability and my subconscious mind will guide me to writing a great novel." Your suggestions can be invented to fit anything you want to do, or anything you want to attract into your life.

4. Write down your main dream or goal at least once a week, and keep it where you can see it every day. Keep reviewing it in your mind until it becomes second nature to you and you really *believe it can come true.*

5. Sit quietly for ten minutes a day and pass through your imagination mental pictures of yourself doing things you really want to do, such as singing, acting, being in your own business, living in a new house, buying a car, taking a long trip. The important thing is to keep reviewing the picture in detail, until it is such a big part of your consciousness that your subconscious will take it up and make it come to pass.

A woman who came to my lectures in Carnegie Hall came to me during World War II, when it was difficult to get a piano. She told me she had no money with which to buy a piano, and she asked me how she should use this study to go about obtaining a piano so that her six year old son who showed musical talent could study this instrument. I told her of this subconscious method of imagining the piano in her apartment, to see it in the room, to visualize her son playing the piano, to look up teachers suitable to teach him; to act as though she already had it. Then I told her to get the thought out into the atmosphere; to tell everyone she knew about her desire to obtain a piano, and to ask their help in obtaining one.

She told a neighbor of hers about this desire, and a week later a friend of the neighbor called her and told her she had an old upright piano she would give her if she paid for the cartage! She obtained the piano for nothing. The subconscious mind will direct you to do the thing, say the word, write the letter that will lead you to the fulfilment of the desire you hold within your mind.

8

The Million Dollar Consciousness
that Brings Success

How often you hear people say, "If I only had a million dollars—what I wouldn't do!"

Everyone has at some time in his life vaguely imagined himself coming into a million dollars, and yet, most people have only a vague idea of what it really is to have a million dollars.

I once told a student of mine, who asked me if my philosophy could teach him how to make a million dollars, "If you can truly build a million dollar consciousness, I can assure you that you will make it."

He replied, "Oh, that'll be easy. Show me how, and I'll rush right home and begin."

I then told this eager young man to go home that night and build a Million Dollar consciousness first. To his question as to how he should do this, I told him to cut out of newspapers with a pair of scissors, a million pieces of paper, equivalent to a dollar each, and to stack them up, after counting them, until he really knew what a million dollars was.

He promised that he would do this at once, and I told him to come back a week later and report his progress to me.

When he returned the following week I noticed that he had a piece of adhesive on his right thumb and forefinger. I asked him how far he had progressed in his task, and he replied, "I cut out two thousand pieces of paper shaped like dollar bills, then I got so exhausted, and my fingers hurt so, that I quit."

I remarked, "If you did not have the patience to cut out one million pieces of paper, how do you think you can possibly create a million dollars? Your consciousness at present is not much more than two thousand dollars."

Most People Fear Big Sums

It's true that no one can have a million dollar consciousness unless he builds it in his mind first. To visualize a million dollars is almost impossible for the average person. Most people are afraid to think in terms of big sums, great achievement, and big fortunes.

In back of every really big fortune, I have discovered, there is first a big money consciousness. Instead of trying to make a million right away, it is vitally important that you start with small things first, and after you have built your awareness of what a million dollars really is, then try for the bigger fortune.

If you are afraid to think in terms of big money, begin today to change your consciousness. Gradually begin to visualize yourself having more and more money, until you lose your fear of big sums. Remember, it takes just as much mental energy to produce a failure in life as to produce a success. The same tools are required; the same mind, the same physical energy, the same emotions. The only difference is one of consciousness. To produce poverty and failure, you need only concentrate mentally on negative thoughts of defeat, failure, and poverty. To create a million dollar consciousness you must use that mental and emotional energy in a positive way and begin to visualize the success you want to achieve.

Why Lincoln's Brother Failed

Abraham Lincoln had a brother who once wrote him, asking for a sizeable loan, and pleading that the land he was farming in Illinois was barren and unproductive and he wished to move elsewhere. Lincoln wrote back telling him that if he could not make a success where he was, there was little likelihood he would succeed elsewhere. Lincoln told his brother that fortune was created by a man's desire to work, his vision for the future, and his willingness to be patient until he could achieve his dream.

The truth of Lincoln's statement was borne out later, by the fact that Illinois became one of the richest states in the Union, producing oil, farm products, industry, and vast riches beyond anyone's wildest dreams. What Lincoln's brother lacked was the Million Dollar Consciousness.

The Will to Succeed

The will to succeed must be firmly implanted in your mind if you wish to attain any degree of fortune. When this will is present, the human mind will seek out the knowledge and the means to achieve that fortune.

An instance of this type of will to succeed was that of a man who worked with Howard Johnson in the early days to make his chain of restaurants a success. This man had a small cart and he sold ice cream on the street. Johnson approached him to deliver his ice cream to his four stores in Boston. He signed a contract with Howard Johnson to deliver ice cream to all his stores for a period of many years.

Soon this man had two trucks delivering Howard Johnson ice cream. Later it expanded into a fleet of ten or more. As the Howard Johnson success spread to encompass hundreds of restaurants, the truck concession which Johnson had given him became extremely valuable. In time, Johnson bought back the contract he had given the delivery man for *Seven Million Dollars!* This man then went into other businesses and today is worth many millions of dollars.

You may start with only a small cart, as this man did, but if you have the will to succeed, and are patient enough, you can gradually build your consciousness into a million dollar one and make a fortune. This applies to any kind of business that you go into.

One man's faith in rubber made him a fortune; Liggett's faith in drugs brought him millions; Sears Roebuck had faith in merchandise, Edison had faith in his inventions, Marconi, in his wireless, Ford in motor cars, Woolworth in cheap products for a dime; the list is long of those who had faith in their products, and built their Million Dollar Consciousness before they achieved their fortune.

Never too Old or too Young

Many people are afraid to think in terms of a big fortune or big ideas that could make them a million because they say, "Oh, I'm too old to begin making a fortune." Still others say, "I'm too young to do anything great or have a fortune." To all such people I say, "You're never too old or too young to begin to build a Million Dollar Consciousness."

History shows that some of life's greatest successes have been those who were very young, and others who were very old. Colonel Vanderbilt built his greatest fortune after he was seventy years of age.

Bernard Baruch became Presidential Advisor and a great financier in his late sixties and seventies, and he has achieved a notable position in the political world with his great wisdom.

Oliver Wendell Holmes was still writing expert legal opinions in his nineties, and served on the Supreme Court bench until he was in his late eighties. The same was true of Justice Felix Frankfurter, who retired in his late eighties, only for reasons of health.

Titian painted his greatest masterpieces after the age of eighty, and Michaelangelo did his work in the Sistine Chapel after he had reached the age of seventy-five.

A more recent example is that of Grandma Moses, who did not even begin painting until she was seventy-six. She made over a million dollars before her death at the age of one hundred and one.

On the other hand, some of the world's greatest discoveries in science, invention and industry have been by those who were still in their twenties and thirties.

Newton was only twenty-four when he discovered the Law of Gravity.

McCormick was in his early twenties when he invented the reaper.

Teddy Roosevelt became the youngest President of the United States in his early forties.

Byron, Keats, Shelley, Shakespeare, were all comparatively young when they did their greatest literary work.

There are no limitations of age or condition for those who first build the Million Dollar Consciousness.

This does not mean that you necessarily want to make a million dollars, for many people are satisfied with a smaller fortune and a lesser degree of success and fame, but if you build your consciousness in terms of thinking **big figures,** it is more than likely that you will achieve a degree of success and fortune in keeping with your consciousness.

Steps to Take for Building Million Dollar Consciousness

1. Get in the habit of thinking in terms of big money. To do this, get a note book and begin to list large sums of money in relation to yourself, such as "Property I Wish to Own." Mortgages, stocks and bonds; money in savings banks; automobile upkeep; house upkeep, income from various sources; personal property. Build this Scrapbook of Destiny, so it becomes real in your mind, until you lose your fear of big sums of money.

2. Make it a habit to study the financial papers and stock listings in your daily newspapers. Become familiar with the various stocks, go into the stock broker's office occasionally, watch the tape, get in the habit of being in the atmosphere of big money, and successful people, until you can visualize yourself owning stocks and trading in the market. This will remove the fear of unfamiliar things, and make you more conversant with the manipulation of big fortunes.

3. Get a book on arithmetic and familiarize yourself with those sections dealing with interest, mortgages, stocks and bonds, and dividends. Acquaint yourself with figures, and practice multiplying, and doing other sums, until you have acquired facility with figures. Then when it comes time for you to go into various business ventures you will have a familiarity with large sums and will not be afraid of them.

4. Pick a list of the ten leading stocks on the New York Stock Exchange, and write out a complete record of your trading in these stocks over a period of months. Such stocks as U.S. Steel, Standard Oil of Calif. or N.J., IBM, American Telephone and Telegraph, Bethlehem Steel, Chrysler, Ford, General Motors. As you buy and sell these big stocks on paper, note the profit and loss you have, and then total these up at the end of six months. If you acquaint yourself with big thinking in relation to finances, the time and opportunity will come for you to make such investments in reality and you will make your fortune.

Billy Rose, who made some money through his productions at the New York World's Fair, built a big money consciousness. He invested in American Telephone and Telegraph twenty years ago, when the stock was low. He kept buying more and more, and when the stock split, he found himself the possessor of over eighty thousand shares of this stock; the second biggest stock holder in the company. If he had feared big sums, he would never have bought his first share!

5. Indulge the Art of Fantasia; play a game with yourself, in which you build a bigger money consciousness. Write out a blank check for the sum of one thousand dollars, made payable to yourself on some mythical bank. Keep this check where you can see it many times a day. Then, gradually, as you absorb the consciousness of this sum, enlarge the figure; make out a check for five thousand dollars, then for ten or fifteen thousand dollars. The point is to accustom your mind to big figures, a big money consciousness so you do not shrink away from thinking in terms of big fortune.

Mind—Memory—and—Money

Your mind has within itself all the elements it needs to create and build a fortune.

The memory stores up all your concepts about money and these are released, through the sympathetic nervous system, into the actions of your muscles, causing you to do the things that attract money or dissipate it.

When you clear your mind of these negative memory–habits regarding money, and change your concept to a positive one, believing that *money is easy to get and keep,* you will change your mental polarity from a negative one to a positive one, and you will find it easier to make a fortune.

Clear Your Mind of the Following Negative Ideas about Money

1. That it's wrong, wicked or harmful for you to have a fortune. This idea is propagated by those who wish to keep you poor while they grow richer.
2. The belief that money is hard to get. It is hard to get *only if you believe it is.* This belief will keep you from ever having the mental and physical energy to go after a big fortune.
3. That you must be born into a fortune or you can never build one. An error in thinking; our biggest fortunes were built by men who *made their money through their creative ideas and imaginations.*

4. Taxes make it difficult now for anyone to make a million. This is a false belief; since World War II, there have been more millionaires than in any previous period of history.

5. You can get something for nothing in this world. This is an error in thinking; you must give something for everything you get. This can be time, labor, ideas, creative imagination, products, or something else of value.

6. That you cannot get rich if you lack a formal education. Many of our wealthiest men and greatest men have little formal education. Education comes from experience, not from books. Do **not** neglect academic education, if you can get it, but do not bemoan the fact that you had no chance to go to high school or college.

7. That money can only be gotten by dishonest means, and that all wealthy people are crooks. This is an error in thinking. Dishonesty may get a man a fortune, but he will surely lose it. History is filled with stories of the defeats of crooked men. Some instances have existed where men have gotten wealth through dishonest means, but it is rare that they hold it.

8. That big fortunes can only come through discovering oil, gold, uranium, or some other natural commodity. This is wrong, for many of the greatest fortunes have been built around a marketable idea, or some commodity that could be sold. Speculation in the Stock Market has won some men fortunes but it has also lost many men fortunes.

9. That the big things have all been done, all the inventions and business ideas have been discovered, and that it is difficult for one to build a fortune through these means. Some of the world's greatest discoveries will come in our atomic and space age. Look at the wonders created by IBM, and the recently discovered Laser Light. Get into some new field like TV, air conditioning, electronics, or jet planes, and grow with the new and expanding industries.

10. That people are hard to sell. This is a delusion, for people like to buy new products, or new ideas. It is up to you to sell yourself first, have faith in yourself and your products, then have the determination to sell.

9

Unlock God's Universal
Storehouse of Riches

God's universal storehouse of riches may be tapped by an enlightened person when he learns to live under the great cosmic laws of utilization and preservation.

There will always be enough resources to meet man's needs if he uses wisdom in conserving nature's treasures, replenishing the bountiful supply of lumber, and restoring the soil once again to its original productive state by modern scientific methods of fertilizing the soil, rotating the crops and by avoiding soil erosion and depletion.

Man can also protect his natural resources from greed and monopoly; he can avoid polluting the air, the streams, and the seas by following the natural laws of preservation. All wealth ultimately comes from the soil, and man must discover ways for protecting these treasures against selfishness and greed.

Grasp This Mental Concept of Wealth.

Before you can build the million dollar consciousness you must grasp this concept of wealth: know that there are resources in the world you can tap to bring you any degree of wealth you choose.

Resourceful men and women have always created their own opportunities. No matter what situations they were in they believed they could improve their lot in life and they set to work with stupendous faith to utilize whatever they had at hand to build their futures.

The reason that most people remain poor all their lives is because they have been mentally programed to believe that there isn't enough wealth to go around. Our minds have been programed with these thoughts:

> the rich have all the money;
>
> money is the root of all evil (actually, the Bible says, "The love of money is the root of all evil") ;
>
> no honest man can ever get rich;
>
> when poverty comes in the door love flies out the window;
>
> save for a rainy day (why not save for a sunny day?)

We have been told for years that there soon will not be enough food to feed the expanding populations and that there won't be enough lumber to build new homes for these millions of people.

Destroy Once and for All This Myth of Poverty.

These negative concepts about the earth's resources must be banished from your mind before you can build the million dollar consciousness that can bring you riches and abundance.

Let me give you some positive mental programing to erase all the negative concepts you may have built about your chances for becoming wealthy.

The Amazon Basin is still an unexplored region teeming with riches that have not been utilized. There are over twenty thousand different species of trees in the Amazon basin, which is twenty times the number to be found in the United States and Canada. Enough lumber, paper pulp and other products can be obtained from untapped sources to give humanity supplies for many centuries to come. And with proper conservation, reforestation projects, and preservation, these sources of riches can be indefinitely maintained so they will produce enough building material for humanity's need in the future.

The Hidden Wealth of America

When you once program your mind with rich ideas instead of poverty-stricken ones, you will be guided by your higher intuitive mind to the finding of your own personal source of wealth and abundance.

In our own Southwest there is enough desert land which can be reclaimed and irrigated to furnish great numbers of people with a supply of food for generations to come.

With the billions spent on fighting the war in Viet Nam, flying to the moon, or developing the atom bomb, mankind could have converted salt water from the Pacific into fresh water to nourish the desert. The resources of hundreds of billions of dollars which America alone has squandered for war during the past century, could have been channeled to give comfort and luxury to people all over the world for hundreds of years to come. These wasted billions have been given to mankind by an overly generous nature and when man dissipates the wealth in his careless fashion, is it any wonder he suffers from periods of recurring depression and economic insufficiency?

There is No Poverty in Nature—Only Poverty in the Mind!

Realize in your own mind, as you now build the million dollar consciousness, there is actually no poverty in nature; there is poverty only in the human mind!

When you break the mesmeric hold that negative mental programing has built within your mind, you will be able to claim any part of the universal storehouse of riches that you choose for your very own, and you will not be depriving others of their share of the world's wealth. There is enough to go around for all people. No one may keep you from your God-given destiny but **yourself!**

There are Eight Vital Golden Keys to unlock the door to riches, which I want to share with you as part of our Million Dollar Secret. Apply these to your own life, and unlock the doors to God's universal storehouse of riches at once.

1. Imagination, Key to Riches

Man's imagination has been given to him so he could mentally see what he wants to be and do in life. This act of seeing mentally, or picturing the world in which you live, must begin today; start seeing this as an unlimited world, with possibilities on every hand to enrich yourself. Mentally see the opportunities that exist for you to better yourself, all around you.

There are three steps to the Imagination; one is forming the Mental Image of what you want in your life; this is called visualization. The second step is focusing the picture in your mind, so that all the details are crystal clear. You do this by reviewing the picture in your mind until you are able to summon up in one picture all the different details of your imaginative picture. The third step is in projecting the mental image to the outer world of reality.

To work effectively in helping you unlock God's Universal Storehouse of Riches, you must daily visualize yourself being in the situations you desire, and attracting the money, objects, and conditions you wish in your life. You do this by thinking and imagining the things you want as already belonging to you. Then each day, you must focus your mind on the details of these things; if it is a new home you wish to move into, you must focus your mind on the individual rooms, the location of the house, the details of the furnishings; the parties you will give there, the gardens, already planted and in full bloom; everything relating to this projected mental image must be clearly outlined in your mind; for if you do not know these details, how can the Universal Intelligence in the world create them for you?

This process is likened to that of an architect drawing up a blueprint for a house. He must know every detail perfectly that is to be built into that house, otherwise the workmen cannot proceed in an orderly manner to build that house.

Projecting the mental image to the outer world, is very much like a motion picture projector projecting a picture onto a screen; if the picture is clean-cut and sharp on the film, the light will transfer the picture to the screen in sharp focus.

You project your mental pictures to the outer world by taking the necessary steps to make the things you want to happen to you, actually occur in the outer world. For instance, you want to become a great speaker or actor. You mentally visualize yourself before a large audience. You hear their applause, and you have the clear-cut picture of the fame and fortune that can come to you because you are a magnetic performer. But this is **not** enough; your next step must be in projecting this mental image to the outer world.

This projection is done when you begin to practice speaking aloud, by studying diction and vocabulary building, by learning how to act or speak through actually rehearsing your actions a hundred times or more. Then will your mental picture begin to come into focus; then will the Universal Mind that controls your mind reveal the means to translate your mental and physical action into visible fame, and wealth.

2. The Power of Faith

When you are trying to unlock God's universal storehouse of riches, you must have implicit faith that the riches are there for you to tap, and that *you have the ability to do it*.

The Bible says, "All things are possible to him that believeth." Faith is the miracle-worker within the mind that can reach out and heal your body, or which you may tap to materialize things you want in the outer world.

Do not let negative people kill your faith by their statements. They will always tell you that everything has been invented, discovered, written, composed and perfected. They will try to discourage you and weaken your resolve to succeed.

He could have Conquered the World with Faith

Napoleon could have conquered the world if he had had faith. When Robert Fulton discovered the principle of the steamboat, he invented a submarine which could have crossed the Channel and sunk the English fleet. He took this invention to Napoleon and offered it to him, but Napoleon lacked faith in it and so Fulton came to America where he perfected his steamboat. But even when he was ready to go up the Hudson, against the powerful currents of the river, the voices of thousands of people who lined the shores, screamed, "It won't start! It won't start!" When the boat began its journey upstream, the shouting of the crowd still did not stop, only this time they changed their words and screamed as one, "It won't stop! It won't stop!"

No one ever believes anything new or different. No one will discover for you the treasures of the universe and give them to you. No one will recognize your gifts easily, and bring you fame and fortune. You and You alone, must have the faith in yourself, your talents, and your ability to unlock the universal storehouse of riches with these eight golden keys. One of the most important elements of our Million Dollar Secret that I have placed in your hands is the Key of Faith.

Believe in yourself, believe in your destiny. Believe in your dream. Never accept the suggestions of any other person that you give up, that you are a failure, that your ideas are *not* good. The moment you do, your power will instantly fail you, just as a short-circuiting of electric power makes it useless.

3. Resourcefulness

One of the great Golden Keys with which you may unlock the doors to God's universal storehouse of abundance is resourcefulness. A resourceful person will create ways of doing things, even when there seems to be no way open. All the great geniuses of history have been resourceful.

Look around you, in whatever environment you are, and try to find ways by which you could change your work, your environment, or your life, if it is not to your liking.

A woman I knew once had three children, when her husband was killed in an accident. She had to support those small children but after the funeral, there was no money left to pay even the rent for another month. She began to look about her, to see what talents she had that could make money for her. She had one gift, she was a good cook and her pies, cakes and cookies were the envy of her friends.

She observed that in the nearby neighborhood where she lived, where construction crews were at work, the men sat around at noontime, eating their lunches. The idea suddenly came to her to make up warm lunches, featuring her pies and cakes, and to go around to construction jobs at lunch time and feed these men. She borrowed two hundred dollars from a relative, and paid it down on an old, second-hand truck, and at lunch time every day, she drove to these construction jobs and sold her hot lunches and baked goods. In one year's time she had expanded to two trucks, had two helpers, and in two years' time she had four such small trucks working for her. She succeeded because she was resourceful.

Never give up trying, and you'll find that when you use the Golden Key to Resourcefulness, you will succeed in doing the things you want to do.

The Golden Key Used by Edison

When Edison had failed time after time in perfecting his electric light bulb, he never stopped trying to find some substance which would last more than a few seconds in the filaments of his lamps. He was so resourceful that he tried thousands of different substances, and each time he failed. But still he did not give up. One day his assistant became so discouraged that he said, "Mr. Edison you've tried ten thousand times and failed, why don't you give up?"

Edison replied, "No I can't give up. Now we know ten thousand things that won't work." And in his next experiment he found something that *did work!*

4. The Golden Key of Enthusiasm

An enthusiastic mind is a young mind. This is a quality of youth. When you lack ability to be enthusiastic about anything, then this shows that you are old in your thinking.

You can build enthusiasm by finding new interests in life. The doors to the universal storehouse of riches are opened by this golden key. Make it a point to find new interests in your work, in your hobbies, in your home. Be constantly interested and excited about life. Have an expanding program of activities which encompasses travel, social and cultural pursuits, new hobbies and sports, church and club activities. Learn to share your interests with your family, and friends, for enthusiasm is contagious.

You must enjoy your work and be enthusiastic about it if you wish to succeed. If you want to progress in business, you should get into something that you can be enthusiastic about. Every great person I have ever met, who achieved the rich rewards of life, had tremendous enthusiasm for the particular things he was doing. Writers, composers, actors, great musicians, men and women in medicine, scientific research, industry—all these who have ever become well-known, successful and rich, were people who brought tremendous enthusiasm to their work.

If you are not happy in the work you are doing, you cannot be enthusiastic about it, and you should make a change as soon as possible. If you are selling a product you do not have faith in, and are not enthusiastic about it, find some other product to sell and it will make you your fortune.

5. Courage

It takes real courage to break with the negative thinking of the world and go contrary to all known opinion about things that concern your destiny. The moment you begin to apply these principles of thinking to your life, to wrest from the universe the fame, fortune and recognition you desire, you will find that it takes tremendous courage to adhere to your principles and beliefs.

Everyone who has ever achieved any notable breakthrough in science, invention, industry or finance, has had to go against the preconceived notions of his day.

An instance in history where one courageous man broke with the thinking of the past and changed the course of history was that of Galileo. From the time of Aristotle, for a period of two thousand years, millions of men had lived and died believing that the earth was the center of our solar system. They had also believed that a heavy object fell to earth quicker than a light object.

When Galileo dared to challenge these two theories, the heads of the University at Padua, and the church leaders, got together and threatened him with excommunication from the church if he did not recant his heresy at once.

Galileo went to the tower of Pisa with a friend, and suspended two objects from strings from the tower; one light, the other heavy. His friend watched on the ground, while Galileo cut the strings holding the two objects. The friend reported that both objects hit the earth at the same moment. Galileo then took his new knowledge to the professors at the University, but no one would believe him. Then when he invented a double convex lens through which he observed craters on the moon, the professors and church heads wouldn't even look through what they called "the devil's instrument." Galileo was forced to recant his theories, but it took courage to even admit of them in those days of darkness and ignorance.

Courage to Discover Life's Secrets

Courage is something that must be built by degrees. You must have mental courage, moral courage and physical courage. Go forth each day and face the problems that arise. Master one thing at a time before going on to another. Never accept the limitations that the world will try to impose on you, for as in Galileo's time, the world is still filled with people who are tied to the old ideas, the old superstitions; who lack the courage to explore the new possibilities there are in the universe for bold and daring conquests. All the new frontiers have not been conquered yet. There are challenges in life which you must meet, if you wish to succeed in your business, social or personal life. You can wrest from the universe more than a good living if you are fortified with courage to dare do the impossible.

It takes great courage to force yourself to undertake new and different ways of doing things. If you seek a new job or want to go into a business of your own, you must take decisive steps, not fearing consequences. The chances are that this Golden Key to the storehouse of riches will open many new doors for you. If you do not succeed at first, then more courage will cause you to continue trying until you do succeed.

6. Curiosity, the Tool of Geniuses

Every genius who has ever made an important discovery or accomplished anything great in human achievement, has used this Golden Key of Curiosity. It was the trait that made Burbank seek to discover new ways of growing fruits, vegetables and flowers and perfecting nature's products for the good of mankind.

Curiosity has been the Golden Key that has given more scientists their great discoveries in nature than almost any other trait. A man's curiosity brought about one of the most revolutionary discoveries in the history of medicine. A doctor put some bread in water to get a culture, which he fed bacteria. One day he discovered that the mold on the bread had turned green, and he was about to throw it away, when his curiosity got the better of him. He fed this mold to some pathological bacteria that he had in a test tube to see what would happen. The next day he looked into the tube to see what had happened, and he observed that all the germs were dead.

He did this for several days, feeding his green mold to thousands of different types of deadly germs, and in each instance the mold killed the bacteria. Thus, through Fleming's curiosity the life-saving miracle-drug penicillin was discovered.

Nature yields her priceless treasures to the person who has an inquiring mind. Look all about you and see how you could improve your situation in life. Look about you in your work and see how many things you can improve. Then mentally become curious about such things as wealth, finances, the fortunes that people have built through their ideas, inventions and discoveries. See how many of their mental processes you can apply, and duplicate, which might improve your own situation in life.

Benjamin Franklin Tapped the Universal Storehouse of Riches

Benjamin Franklin had enormous curiosity; he did everything he could to probe God's universal storehouse of riches, and through his discoveries and inventions he benefited all mankind enormously. His experiments with the key and the kite, proved the existence of electricity in the atmosphere and paved the way for Edison's wonderful discoveries in that field. He invented the first bi-focal glasses through discovering the secret of fusing two pieces of glass together. One day he wanted to invent a coat that people might wear in the hot, humid tropics; something that would not absorb heat, but repel it. He was sitting in his home one wintery day, looking out at the thick blanket of snow that covered the earth. His curiosity got the best of him, and he decided to perform an experiment to determine which would absorb more heat, black or white objects.

Franklin took two pieces of cardboard, one white, the other black, and laid them side by side on the snow, in the sunlight. Hours later he went out and looked at them. The black paper had sunk deeply into the snow, the white sheet was still practically on the surface. Franklin shrewdly deduced that the black paper had absorbed more of the sun's rays than the white, and that white would be the best color to use to repel the heat of the sun. That discovery led to changes in roofing, and now we see people using aluminum, and white surfaces to keep places cool in the hot summer.

7. Using Your Time Intelligently

Everything you will ever have in life depends on time and timing. Nature's priceless treasures can be tapped easier if you know how to use your time intelligently. There are only twenty-four hours in a day. Eight hours are spent in working, eight hours in sleeping, and this leaves eight precious hours to do with as you wish. Two hours of that time is spent, as a rule, in relaxing, reading, going to movies, looking at TV, and another two or three hours is usually spent in eating, or shopping. So that time that is usable actually dwindles down to about two or three hours a day. It is the way you use this extra time that often determines the degree of success you shall have in the future.

We cannot make more time, but we *can wisely use the time available to us.* Edison was so eager to use time for his inventions that he made it a practice to sleep only four hours a night. You can gain many more precious hours of life by conserving your time, and avoiding doing anything wasteful. How many hundreds of inferior movies have you sat through? How many hundreds of hours of time have you wasted on frivolous TV programs, when you could have been using that precious time to study a valuable book that would have improved your mind, or to go to a course in evening high school where you could have taken some study that would have prepared you for a new career. The wasted hours we spend are the very ones that we should have used constructively to win success and make a fortune.

You need social contacts, it's true, you need some relaxation and rest, some golfing, and bowling, but *most people spend most of their spare time in these aimless pursuits,* and have no extra time to give to self-improvement and advancement.

Queen Elizabeth the First is reported to have said on her death bed, "I would give my entire kingdom for one more moment of time!" Time is the substance of which nature weaves the golden stuff of life. It is money, it is ideas, it is wealth; you have been given only a certain amount of this priceless gold of life—use your time wisely, and you will profit thereby.

8. Making the Right Decisions

One of the greatest forces for unlocking the universal storehouse of riches is that of making the right decision. Remember, the gold, the oil, the diamonds, the coal, the lumber are all in existence in the universe. Nature's gifts and treasures are all there, waiting for man's joyous discovery and acceptance. What keeps man from achieving the more abundant life? It is very often due to the fact he cannot *make a decision as to what he wants or what he wants to do.* The right decision is even more difficult to make, for there are always so many paths open for one to take.

How do you make a decision? You must sit down with a pencil and paper and write down at the head of the sheet, the decision you must make. For example, let us take a hypothetical illustration: *Should I stay in New York or move to California?* Then list on one side, which you mark debit, the things against taking such a move; and on the other side under credit, write down the reasons why you should make the move. Put down everything you can possibly think of consciously *for* and *against* your making that vital decision. Then sit quietly in the silence for a few moments, and let your mind review all the reasons why you should or shouldn't make the move. Something within your own mind, which science calls the Higher Mind, the faculty of intuition will now begin to take over. This higher mind will gently nudge you in one direction or the other. You must be especially sensitive to this higher intelligence, and recognize it when it is trying to send you on a definite course. The evidences are rather obvious; you will feel a deep urge to do a thing; you will try to decide against it, and this higher mind will keep bringing your mind back again and again to the course of action it knows is best for you. *When this idea persists for hours or days then it is the right decision.* Follow it unerringly. What if it should prove wrong? It seldom will, but if it should, it is better to *make some decision,* even a wrong one, than to sit without making a decision and vegetate the rest of your life.

The One Decision that Made one Man a Million

Early in his career Bernard Baruch was forced to make an important decision that could have broken him or made him a million. He had carefully built up the sum of thirty-five thousand dollars from a small amount he had, through the stock market. He heard men talking in the stock market about Delaware and Western stock. He bought it to sell short; that is, if the stock went down, he would make big money, but if it went up, he would lose money.

The very next day the stock went up four points. He had to make a decision at that moment as to whether to get out then, and suffer a small loss, or ride with the stock until it broke and went down, which would make him a fortune.

He sat quietly, meditating all during that day of his vital decision, and he kept the stock. Late that afternoon when he went out, he saw newspaper headlines telling that Delaware and Western Railroad had gone down twenty-five points, and Baruch had made a million dollars on his holdings! His decision paid rich dividends, and it was the beginning of his vast future fortune.

How David Sarnoff's Decision Made a Fortune

David Sarnoff, Chairman of the Board of the giant RCA corporation, had to make a vital decision when CBS came out with color TV some years ago. Sarnoff decided to produce color TV for RCA, against the judgment of other members of the company. Sarnoff stuck to his decision, and for eight long years the company lost money becauseof his color TV. Sarnoff had faith that his color was better than that of CBS, and in the face of tremendous opposition he stuck by his guns. Soon his big decision paid off, for RCA made the biggest profit it had made in years, and all because of color TV. If Sarnoff had given up and *not* stuck by his vital decision, the whole course of destiny for RCA might have been changed.

Ability to Make Quick Decisions

The ability to make quick decisions shows an alert and highly sensitive mind. You can develop this ability. Pick imaginary situations, that you might experience in life; write them down, then go over all the possible courses of action you might take, and pick the *one that you consider best.*

Here are a few samples one might come across in life. Try to make your decision as quickly as possible, after going over the situation and then consider several alternatives that are presented.

Illustration No. 1. A woman has a husband who is alcoholic. She has two young children. The husband is abusive and threatening when drunk. The wife fears bodily harm and even death. She must make a decision. Which of the following should she make?

1. Take the two children and leave the husband, going to live with relatives.
2. Appeal to the authorities to put her husband away as being mentally defective?

3. Stick it out, trying to change her husband and risking bodily harm to her children and herself.

Illustration No. 2. An employee has been with a firm for several years and has always been considered trustworthy. It is found that he has been taking money from the company and concealing it. You, as head of the firm must make a decision. Which would you make?

1. Call the police and accuse the man of theft?
2. Discuss the matter with the employee, giving him a chance to make restitution for the money taken?
3. Fire the person immediately, refusing to give references for another job?

Illustration No. 3. You have just won the Irish Sweepstakes, and you have won over 100,000 dollars. Which of these three decisions would you make?

1. Go to Ireland to collect, thus avoiding giving the U.S. Government about a third of your winnings? This decision would mean living in Ireland all the rest of your life.
2. You would invest the money in stocks and bonds and try to double it?
3. You would put the money in real estate and wait for it to grow in value?

Illustration No. 4. A woman has four small children. She discovers her husband has been having an affair with another woman. When confronted by his wife he swears he does not love the other woman. Should the wife:

1. Forgive him and continue to remain with him for the sake of their four children?
2. Should she demand a divorce and custody of the children, with a fair financial settlement?
3. Should she continue living with her husband, in appearance only, for the sake of the children, not getting a divorce, but concealing the true facts from her family and friends?

Test Your Skill and Make Your Own Decisions

When you test your skill in these hypothetical cases, it will help you readily make your own decisions in important matters. Psychologists say that it is better to make a wrong decision than to let your mind vacillate in uncertainty between two possible courses of action. The mind that is able to make quick decisions is generally able to take advantage of opportunities in the business world that arise suddenly. I knew one man in California who had a chance to buy land on famous Wilshire Boulevard during the depression years for a small sum. He couldn't make his decision, and the boom that came after World War II in real estate would have made him millions. He is still living in comparative poverty, and his opportunities have passed him by all his life because he couldn't make decisions.

Decide to buy that house you have considered for such a long time. It will force you to make more money to meet the payments and some day you will own it. It may increase in value and pay you back in years to come more than you invested.

Now is the time to buy that stock you are considering. The market may go up and you will make a fortune. If it goes down, you can cover yourself with a stop-sale, and limit your losses.

Now is the best time to go into business. Make your decision, then go into that business with faith that it will succeed. Many people have weathered the storms of those first years in a new business to go on to achieve a fortune.

Now is the time to take that course in cosmetology, singing, acting, writing, public speaking, business administration—if you wait too long time will pass you by. Make your decision and stick with it. It will give you more strength of character to make that decision and stick with it!

Nine Ways to Increase Your Riches

1. Look about you, wherever you are, and see how you can improve your circumstances. There are many untapped resources in your environment; find these and release the frozen assets you already have. Are you getting enough use out of your present car, your refrigerator, your vacuum cleaner, your business equipment? Many

times throughout a lifetime you can increase your riches
by utilizing fully the things you already possess. If you
rush out and buy new equipment, a new car, new wash-
ing machines or refrigerators, you spend enough money
in a period of twenty years to go into some business
where you can be independent.

2. Do you have goods that are lying about, which you no
    longer use, but which represent capital? Many people
    have things in storage, in attics and basements, in their
    workshops which they should gather together and liqui-
    date for cash. These objects lie around and depreciate
    every year, until they are worthless. Cash in everything
    you actually do not need and have not used for a period
    of one or two years.

3. Do you have a marketable product or a unique service
    which you have not commercialized? If you have, you
    should concentrate your mind and efforts on making it
    pay off, instead of searching in unfamiliar fields for
    riches you cannot achieve.

4. Are you utilizing the contacts you already have to increase
    your abundance and supply? If you are a real estate or
    insurance salesman, for instance, you may already have
    ready-made prospects among your circle of friends and
    acquaintances. Do not hesitate in approaching them as
    prospects; they will be glad to give you their business
    rather than go to a stranger. Many lawyers, doctors and
    other professional people build their practice on such
    social contacts. Also utilize the capital, labor and ideas
    of friends who give you suggestions for partnerships
    and other ventures in which you can avail yourself of
    their valuable training and background.

5. Do you avail yourself of the many free services that your
    government gives? You may write to the printing office
    in Washington, D.C. and obtain free information and
    literature on everything from chicken raising for profit,
    to gold-mining and homesteading free land in the great
    Southwest. You can obtain important information on
    subjects that could make you a fortune. One man I
    know did this and obtained vital information on mush-
    room growing; he had exactly the space and the re-

quirements in his cool, damp basement to begin this
venture and now has a hundred-thousand-dollar-a-year
flourishing business supplying fine restaurants and hotels with his choice products. I know still other cases
where people are raising mink, still others, shipping
lobsters and other types of fish products all over the
U.S. They began with just such government information as I am suggesting.

6. You can increase your present income and stretch each
   dollar, instead of trying to make more and more, by
   taking advantage of all the many free entertainments
   and public functions that are presented in almost every
   city and town throughout America. Check with your
   local town hall for such free lectures, travelogues, adventure movies, and special industrial films put out by
   such big companies as American Telephone Co., U.S.
   Steel, IBM and many other organizations who lend
   these films free to various civic groups. There are fine
   dramas being presented by local high schools and col-
   leges; art and musical events presented with talented
   pupils in conservatories; free lectures in churches and
   such organizations as P.T.A., Lions Clubs, Rotary
   Groups, Veteran Groups, American Legion, Daughters
   of the American Revolution, and other organizations.
   They often present dances, charity bazaars, church so-
   cials, picnics, and other activities, which you may par-
   ticipate in at little or no cost. These *free* programs put
   money into your pocket, for they save on entertainment
   expenses, and in a twenty year period this can amount
   to several thousand dollars.

7. Check the Patent Office for products that are being pat-
   ented, or patents that have run out. These may give
   you ideas for inventions of your own that could make
   you a fortune. You may obtain literature on this subject from the Patent Office in Washington, D.C.

   Also check on books that might have movie possibilities; especially if they are unsuccessful as novels.
   Generally such first novels by authors can be bought for
   a small figure; then you will own the movie rights and
   can sell them to movie companies.

One instance I know where a young man did this was that of the novel, "The Cup and Sword," a first novel by a young woman. A young man who used to come to our lectures read this novel, and got the idea it would make a good movie. He held this thought in his mind until he got the bright idea of buying the movie rights. He sought out the author and obtained the movie rights for only $500 which he agreed to pay in the future. He then went to Universal-International studios with his product and sold it. This young man became the producer of the picture, and Rock Hudson was his star. The name of the finished picture was, *This Earth Is Mine.* The young man, still in his late twenties, became a big producer.

8. Investigate option buying, a principle used by the noted real estate promoter and speculator, William Zeckendorf. He obtains an option on property, and then tries to sell it at an enormous profit, before his option is up. He has made hundreds of millions this way. He is reputed to have made over seven million dollars on a Park Avenue property where the old Hotel Marguery used to be.

9. Many thousands of people go on in conditions of lack and limitation, needing medical or dental or eye care, and not receiving it because they are too poor to go to specialists in these fields. Such a woman came to my lectures in Carnegie Hall some years ago. She told me one day, after listening to a lecture on demonstrating money to obtain things she wanted, that she wanted a thousand dollars, but didn't know how to go about getting it with this philosophy.

I asked her what she wanted the money for. She told me her sister needed a delicate operation on her eyes which would cost a thousand dollars, if a specialist did the surgery needed.

I told her to change her thinking; to stop thinking in terms of one thousand dollars, which was a barrier, and to call an eye clinic where the greatest surgeons operate and give their services free to the needy. She did this, and obtained the services of the biggest man in that field, and it didn't cost her sister a cent!

Many times you or your family may obtain benefits under social security, pension plans, veteran's rights, and this can include education for your children, health and medical benefits, hospitalization free of charge, and various sums of money. Check your status with your local health and welfare groups, and with the Social Security administration in your city, to see if you or your family are eligible for such benefits. Many veterans' families come under this category, especially if the man died in service.

10

Duplicate the Power of
Great Men of History

If you wish to be great and make your fortune, learn how to duplicate the power of the greatest men and women in history. These men discovered The Million Dollar Secret, some of them by accident, others through inspiration or sheer dint of hard work and persistent effort.

There are three things that will make you outstanding in any business field, and these three things were present in the works of all great geniuses:

1. The ability to know your own talents and possibilities.
2. Daring to attempt to do the seemingly impossible.
3. The courage to persist in the face of obstacles.

The Universal Mind that You can Tap

There is a Universal Mind that works through all men, which you may tap when you want to draw on it for power, new ideas, guidance in your affairs, for new gifts and talents. This great Universal Mind is the same one that the outstanding men and women of history used to carry them to great heights.

This Universal Mind knows the secret of what makes an acorn turn into a giant oak. It is the intelligence in the hen's egg that knows how to make a perfect chick in a short time. It is the intelligence in the soil that knows how to draw nourishment from the earth and create a rose or a cabbage from the same elements in the soil.

Pick the Great Ones You Wish to Emulate

In the list below I have given a few of the great ones of history who have accomplished worthwhile things. You may pick these people to use as outstanding examples to imitate. Study their lives and works, and then let the Higher Mind that is within you, show you how you may also do the great things you desire.

In philosophy, study the works of such men as Aristotle, Plato, Socrates, Spinoza, and Emerson. Emulate the greatness of their thinking, and accept their universality of thought, the theories they advance, the transcendental philosophy of beauty, goodness, and truth, which they advocate. Your mind will grow and expand under the impetus of their high-voltage thinking.

In psychology, study the works of Freud, Jung, William James, Havelock Ellis, and learn their secret power of greatness. Let your life reflect their teachings, their knowledge, their broad vision.

In science, study the works of Pasteur, Burbank, Einstein, Galileo, Newton, and let their revelations and achievements be an inspiration to you to achieve greatness in your own field.

In the field of invention, study the lives of Edison, Eli Whitney, Robert Fulton, McCormick, the Wright Brothers. Let their daring, vision, foresight and courage infuse your mind with the spirit of adventure. Set out to discover the secrets of the universe by using these great minds as beacon lights to show you the way.

In the field of music, call upon the same Universal Mind within you, that motivated the minds of such illumined, creative souls as Mozart, Beethoven, Chopin, Strauss and Wagner, and you will also create magnificent music, if that is your soul-bent. In the modern field choose such examples as Cole Porter, Gershwin, Irving Berlin, Rodgers and Hammerstein, and others you especially admire. Let them be the examples which you study and emulate. Use only the inspiration of these great souls, and then try to be original, doing only that creative work which fits your own soul-pattern and rhythm.

In art, duplicate the inspiration of some of the classical painters that the whole world reveres; Michaelangelo, Raphael, Titian, Tintoretto, Van Dyck, Leonardo da Vinci, and Rembrandt. Dupli-

cate their technical perfection, their unity and harmony of line
and color, their originality, and beauty.

In literature, choose the inspired writers who have elevated the
standards of the world, such authors as Shakespeare, Milton, Hugo,
Balzac, Dickens, Shelley, Keats, Byron, Hawthorne, Poe, and Long-
fellow. Let their works and ideas inflame your mind with a desire
to create beauty for the world in your own literary efforts.

In politics, emulate the ideals and great thoughts of Webster,
Jefferson, Lincoln, Washington, and Hamilton. These men all had
noble, humanitarian thoughts and are worthy of study and emulation.

In industry and finance you should strive to emulate the pattern
of thinking that has brought success to some of our greatest industrialists and financiers. Study the lives of the following men, strive
to emulate their thoughts, assemble the facts that you will need to
carry you high in the financial world, and then let the Universal
Mind that brought these men success, also work through your
mind, bringing you a fortune.

Rockefeller, Vanderbilt, Morgan, Ford, Kaiser, Chrysler, and
Astor, are just a few of the great wizards of industry and finance
you should know about. Strive to duplicate their imaginative feats,
their progressive ideas, their daring, their big concepts and bold
actions. Study their organizational ability, their expansive, for-
ward-looking minds, their good judgment.

In the theatrical world there are outstanding performers, directors, producers, singers, actors, and writers, who will give you rich
rewards if you study their lives and attempt to duplicate their
inspiration and genius. The lives of Bernhardt, and Duse, the
genius of Shakespeare and Ibsen, the technique and polish of John
Barrymore and Laurence Olivier, the greatness of Belasco and
Ziegfeld, the audacity of Zanuck and De Mille, the modern drama
of a Tennessee Williams and a William Inge, or Edward Albee.
The genius of a Disney...all these great minds can contribute
something to your total concept of power and brilliance in the
theatrical world.

Choose Your Gift. Then Act

Find the field in which you are most interested; study the lives
of those who have achieved greatness in your particular field, then
choose your gift and act! With the dream within your mind, you

are half-way on the road to achievement, but you must *act to materialize your dream.* The Chinese have a saying: "A journey of a thousand miles begins with but a single step."

That first step of choosing what you want, letting your desires guide you to the path you wish to take, is probably one of the most important that you can take in applying our Million Dollar Secret to your own life and success.

Step by Step to Greatness

1. Pick the field you wish to specialize in; learn all you can about it, study the lives of the persons who have had outstanding success in that field, then strive to emulate their pattern of thinking. If you wish to be a doctor, study the lives of the great scientists and specialists in medicine; if it is law you are interested in, become acquainted with the lives of the great lawyers of the past, and see how they succeeded. If you want to become a great scientist, an architect, inventor, or industrialist, make it a point to study their lives, see how they accomplished their great things, then emulate them.

2. Each day strive to put into action one or more of the qualities or traits that you have learned from the lives of great men. Imitate these thoughts, if need be, at first, then you will gradually begin to originate great thoughts and actions of your own.

3. Take specialized training to perfect your gifts and talents. Assemble facts about the work you choose; see the good and bad sides, then, if you are still interested, let no one divert you from your goal.

4. Let what I call Divine Discontent motivate you in your desire to achieve perfection. Never be satisfied with your present accomplishments or progress. When you are satisfied you cease to grow. Everything in nature is in a constant state of flux, from an imperfect to a more perfect state. Constantly desire change and evolvement, for this is the Law of Action that will help you constantly evolve higher and higher in the future.

5. Aim for the stars, even though you may not achieve them, at least such an ambitious mind will assure you of reaching some kind of high goal. The incentive for aiming high must come from within, your desire to achieve greatness. Browning said, "Ah, but a man's reach should exceed his grasp, / Or what's a heaven for?"

6. Create a vortex of mental activity about yourself. Break the

inertia which may be holding you back by doing *something*, almost anything is preferable to sitting back and refusing to make an effort. There is a law in nature which states, "Action and reaction," "Cause and Effect." When you set some action into motion, it must have an instantaneous reaction. There is no cause without its corresponding effect. If you make up your mind you are going to achieve something like playing the piano or doing touch typing, you can hold this idea in mind forever and yet if you do not take some step by action, you will never acquire facility in that field.

7. Never be satisfied with the limitations that life seems to have placed on you and your expression of your talents. Remember, all great men had to break the mould of negativity and limitation to achieve their dreams. The power is within your mind to rise as high as you aspire. If you lack the education, look about you for the means to improve your mind and acquire knowledge. Our vast libraries are filled with the priceless wisdom of the ages; go there and learn how to use your library to best advantage. There are correspondence courses you may take in the privacy of your own home, from high school to college subjects, that can help improve your mind and prepare you for a better position. There are extension courses for adults in all universities, night classes in high school and college; you need never say that you do not have an opportunity to obtain sufficient education to achieve your goal. The means are all about you; search them out and utilize them. Part of our Million Dollar Secret is the building of mental power, so you may better express your God-given gifts and talents.

11

The Million Dollar
Personality that Wins

Some people seem to be born lucky. They grow up in circumstances that seem favorable for their maturing into well-balanced, integrated personalities. They seem to possess charm and attractiveness; everyone seems to like them, and want to help them.

Others are less fortunate, they are born in environments that may be negative and shabby, surrounded by people who are negative, fearful, financially pinched and constantly worried. These people acquire mental habits that are difficult to break in adult life.

Epictetus said of habit, "Every habit and faculty is preserved and increased by correspondent actions, as the habit of walking, by walking; or running, by running."

The more you practice thinking or doing a thing, the easier it becomes, until finally, by building positive mental habits, you are able to perform consistently at a high level of action in the expression of your personality.

You live in a world surrounded by people. These people can help or hinder you, depending on whether they like or dislike you. This is a fact that is impossible to overlook. To achieve the fulfilment of your goal, it will be easier for you to develop the Million Dollar Personality that Wins than to go through life constantly fighting the opposition and enmity of people who take an active dislike to you.

Of course, it is impossible to make every person you meet like you, but there are certain basic rules psychologically, which can ensure you of having a forceful, magnetic and likeable personality.

Choose the Type of Person You Want to Be

It is possible for you now to choose the type of person you want to be, just as you choose the suit or dress you want to wear. Psychologists tell us that we are conditioned by our own minds through suggestions and opinions we hold, or tell ourselves.

If you constantly tell yourself you are inferior, you will gradually begin to take on the hang-dog appearance of an inferior person. You will shrink back from contact with people. They will sense your reactions and shy away from you.

If you make it a point to re-inforce your ego by telling yourself you are worthy of the best life has to offer, and that you are likeable, pleasant, happy and loving towards others, people will instantly feel your power and gravitate to you.

Building a magnetic personality is easy, when you once know how. It is a matter of satisfaction to be able to win friends and hold them, but it has intrinsic value also that can be counted in actual dollars and cents. Tests taken by psychologists proved that men and women who had studied their personalities and worked to perfect and polish them actually got more jobs as executives than those who had inferior personalities but great ability. If it comes to a choice between a pleasant, cheerful, happy-appearing person, for a job, and one who is morose and sullen all the time, ability being equal, the pleasant person will be selected every time!

"Smile, Shirley, Smile!"

I remember once I went out to Fox studios years ago to do an interview with Will Rogers and on our way to the commissary we passed through a large sound stage where a director was taking a test of a six year old girl. We stopped for a moment to watch the talented youngster. Finally she stopped her song and dance and would not go on; a childish pout was on her face, and the director appealed to the mother, who stood on the sidelines, to do something about the impasse.

Finally the mother said in a cheerful voice, "Smile, Shirley, smile!" And little Shirley Temple's face lit up in a broad smile and she went on with her song and dance. That screen test won for Shirley Temple a contract that brought her millions of dollars.

Whenever you feel your personality is not up to par, and you feel discouraged or depressed about conditions, stop and think of that story, and say to yourself, "Smile, Shirley, Smile!" It will become the auto-conditioning to your subconscious mind to remember the value of a smile. This does not mean that you must go around grinning vacantly all the time, but when occasion demands you look your best, remember, nothing is as impressive or pleasant on a human being's face as a smile.

The Chinese say, "Man who cannot smile must not open shop."

A smile is magnetic, a frown is unmagnetic. It is as simple as that. It takes more muscles of the face to frown that it does to smile. Stand before your mirror and practice the Million Dollar smile. Let your face be uplifted and illumined by thinking of the happiest experiences you have had in your lifetime, since you were a child.

Now form a habit of holding only these positive, happy thoughts in your mind each day. When you are tempted to go back to the old habit-patterns of thinking negatively, change your thoughts and think of the joyous and happy experiences you have had in your life.

The Importance of Optimism

People can feel your moods, just as they can see the inner man by the outer clothing. When you see a picture of a haunted house in the movies, you see shutters banging, bats flying out of the belfry, chains clang, and a miasmic pall seems to hang over everything; right away you know you are going to view a mystery story.

There is a thought-atmosphere that you can build also, and it tells everyone you meet just what is going on inside your mental house. If you are optimistic, bright and hopeful about things, people feel this instantly. They want you around them if you are an optimist, constantly seeing the bright side of things. A pessimist constantly bemoans his lot in life, and is always talking about negative things that have happened to him, or that he expects to happen to him in the future.

Someone has described a pessimist as being someone who looks at a partly-filled bottle of whiskey and bemoans, "My, that bottle's half empty." Whereas an optimist looks at the same bottle and says, "Glory be! The bottle's half full!"

This difference in your mental attitude can spell the difference between success and failure. It all depends on how you look at life, people, opportunities. Nothing is ever perfect for anyone, but if you acquire the mental knack of seeing life as being replete with opportunities, people as being kind and good, money as being easy to get, you will gradually change your personality from an inferior, pessimistic one to a superior, optimistic one.

The Importance of Being a Good Listener

I once knew a real estate salesman who made hundreds of sales because he learned the secret of being a good listener. Most salesmen who showed property, he noticed, oversold their clients on the merits of the house he was trying to sell. This salesman discovered that people want to express themselves about the house they're planning to buy. He quietly shows them through the house, then leaves them alone for a half hour or so, letting them wander casually from room to room, expressing their private opinions about the good and bad features of the house. This salesman increased his sales tremendously when he learned this million dollar secret of being a good listener.

You will find that most people enjoy talking about themselves and the things that interest them. This may seem selfish, but it is human nature. Knowing this, you can capitalize on it, if your work is in the selling field. Give a person your attentive ear, making suitable comments, and drawing him out. Let him expound on his favorite subjects. The word "I" should be used sparingly, and the personal pronoun "You" used as often as possible. Now, this does not mean you should become a complete mental non-entity, when talking to people, but if it is someone whose interest you wish to win, someone who can advance your interests, someone you are trying to sell, it is vitally important that you talk about him, and *not* about yourself.

How a Courteous Person Made a Fortune

There seems to be little connection between courteous actions and a person's general personality, but let me assure you that this dynamic quality of being courteous can pay rich dividends. Let me tell you of an example from life.

A salesman in a department store noticed a little old lady

dressed in black, who had come into the store on a rainy day. She had no umbrella, and it was obvious she was not interested in buying anything. The salesman had little to do, so he smiled at the little old lady courteously and offered to show her around his department. When the rain had stopped, this young man showed her to a taxi and put her into it, but before going, the lady asked him for his name. He gave it, and promptly forgot the incident.

A few days later a letter arrived for this young man. It stated, "Dear Sir: Recently, my mother came into your store to get out of the rain, and you showed her great courtesy and consideration, which she told me about. I wonder if you would be interested in a business proposition?

"I am in need of a purchaser to go throughout Europe to buy antiques for a castle I am furnishing in Scotland, and I believe your qualifications would be suitable for such a position. Let me know at the earliest possible moment if you would consider this position." The letter was signed "Andrew Carnegie."

This young man accepted the position and in a few years time became Andrew Carnegie's most trusted and valuable employee, making a fortune through this association.

Never let anyone tell you that courtesy and a smile do not pay off!

Another illustration from life was carried in the *New York Times;* it told of a young lady who sat in Central Park during her lunch hour, feeding squirrels and pigeons. She noticed a lonely, old man sitting there every day doing the same thing. She struck up a conversation with him. He learned that she worked nearby and found out her name. For months she was courteous and kind to this lonely man. A year later a lawyer sought her out; this old man had died leaving her an enormous fortune!

Interior and Exterior Decoration for Your Personality

The outer side of your personality that you show the world is important, it's true; cleanliness, good clothing, good grooming, a cheerful, smiling face, a happy expression; these are a part of the Million Dollar Personality, but what of the hidden side of your nature, what I call the interior side of your personality? Your mental attitude towards people and life shows in your outer self.

If this interior is colored by thoughts of unhappiness, fear, failure, worry, hate, and envy and revenge, you will soon reflect these negative mental attitudes to the outer world and drive people away from you. What you habitually think, you become. Someone has said, "God gave rattlesnakes rattles to warn people they are poisonous." God has also given certain outer traits and mannerisms which reveal to the sensitive, intuitive minds of others, what a man's character is really like. These tell-tale signs are shown by the expressions in your eyes, the tightness around your mouth, the evasiveness of your eyes, the downward pull of your lips; shrewdness and cunning stamp itself in the muscular contours of the entire face, giving you away to anyone who has perceptive sense. Most people can accurately gauge another person's character instantly, without even knowing how they do this.

Build these Qualities in Your Mind

To radiate friendliness, trust, confidence, loyalty, cheerfulness, happiness, honesty, goodness, truthfulness, charity, and love to the outer world, carefully build these qualities in the fabric of your thinking. Each day write down on a little card which you carry in your pocketbook, a key word that will determine your mental attitude for that day; take the word **friendliness**. Look at this card several times a day to remind you of the keynote for your mind for that entire day. Determine that all day long you shall be friendly towards other people; look for qualities of friendship in those you meet all day. Sometimes we think of friends as being those who do some great act of kindness for us, or someone who is in a position to help us, but I have found that sometimes people in the most obscure positions had the greatest power to help one, if a person cultivated him. Secretaries and assistants to great men can often prove most helpful in giving you valuable appointments with the head of a firm. I know one man who every Christmas sends gifts to every secretary of every firm he does business with. He has built a million-dollar-a-year business because of these seemingly humble and unimportant men and women!

Wordsworth said it so beautifully in this poem:

Small service is true service while it
   lasts,
Of humblest friends, bright creature!
   scorn not one:

The daisy, by the shadow that it casts,
Protects the lingering dewdrop from
   the sun.

Summary of the Million Dollar Personality

1. Build positive mental habits of your personality; avoid talking or thinking discouragement, despair, disillusionment, and disaster, and concentrate your mind on positive, happy thoughts.

2. Build your ego by suggesting to your subconscious mind that you are likeable, pleasant, happy and loving towards others. Carry out a regime of daily action in which you maintain these mental attitudes in your every day relations with others.

3. When you feel that your personality is not up to par, tell yourself to *sparkle,* and you will instantly change your attitude and show a bright, happy side to the world.

4. Realize the value of a smile and use a smile as often as possible. Avoid frowning for this sets the face in an expression that is unpleasant and unmagnetic.

5. Be optimistic rather than pessimistic; avoid talking about sickness, accidents, failure and unhappy events. Talk of pleasant and happy events, and build your thought-atmosphere so that it reflects only optimism and good cheer to the outer world.

6. Be a good listener when talking to others, giving them a chance to express themselves and talk about things that interest them.

7. Be courteous and kind in your dealings with others; for these two qualities often pay rich dividends.

8. Interior decoration has to do with the coloration of your thoughts on your personality. Keep your thoughts beautiful and inspiring and your outer personality will also be beautiful.

9. Build the qualities of friendliness, trust, confidence, loyalty, cheerfulness, happiness, honesty, goodness, truthfulness, charity and love in your mind and they will decorate your exterior.

10. Be friendly towards even the most humble person, for you never know when they have the power to do some great favor for you that can bring you immeasurable benefits.

12

Ten Steps that can Make
You a Mental Giant

The most tragic excuse given by millions of people who fail in life is, "I never had a chance to finish my education. I only went to eighth grade." Or, in some cases, they claim they went to only one year of high school, or that they didn't graduate from high school.

These people lean on this crutch all their lives, really believing that this lack of a complete formal education is a sufficient reason for their lack of success. Throughout history there are thousands of examples of men and women who had no formal education and yet, they were able to achieve outstanding success. Your brain never stops evolving and expanding, and if you train your mind in the right way, you can truly become a mental giant.

Geniuses have always been able to overcome the limitations and ignorance of their times. Great minds like Galileo, Copernicus, Columbus, Socrates, Aristotle, Michelangelo, Chopin, and, in our own age, Edison, did not accept the limitations of their ages. They absorbed all they could from academic sources, but they did not stop there. They formed new concepts in art, music, philosophy, exploration, science, and inventions that were different from the past and because of this daring to break with tradition, they achieved greatness in their individual fields.

Creative Power that Lies within Your Mind

Creative power lies within your mind to achieve anything you desire. It can be a million dollars you ask for, or it can be a great idea for a novel or screen play, or a musical composition, an invention, a secret formula for some new chemical that could revolutionize medicine or industry. This Creative Power can be stimulated into vibrant action *only* if you take active steps to build your Mental Power. Your mind has enormous capacity to produce anything you ask of it, but you must know the formula for increasing its capacity, building its potentials, releasing its creative fire for whatever you want to do in life.

I claim that anyone can enormously increase his creative mental power and literally become a mental giant, if he applies the ten principles given in this chapter alone. And this, irrespective of the limitations of education. You may still soar to undreamed-of heights if you will apply the Million Dollar Secret and build your mind step by step, to one that holds unlimited concepts.

Remove the Shadows of Doubt and Fear

Before you begin the study of this part of our Million Dollar Secret, I ask that you rid your mind of all doubts and uncertainties, and to *really believe you can do the things I am going to tell you about.* Remove the shadows of fear and doubt and limitation that may fill your mind, and then become imbued with only one thought: *you can do anything you desire!*

Let me tell you of an incident from history of a young man who learned this great secret of Creative Mental Power when he was only sixteen years of age, and how he conquered the world through this knowledge.

An ancient king was reviewing his stable of beautiful Arabian horses late one afternoon, as the sun was about to set on the horizon. His fifteen year old son watched on the sideline. Finally a beautiful white stallion was led forth by the groom and as one of the king's men was about to mount the horse, he began to rear and kick, throwing the man to the ground. The king was angry at his undisciplined action on the part of the animal and ordered that he be destroyed, as he was too dangerous to ride.

The king's son stepped forth from the shadows and pleaded

with his father not to kill the animal. "Give him to me," the boy pleaded. "I know I can tame him."

Grudgingly his father gave his consent, and the boy turned the horse about, mounted him and rode off, much to the astonishment of the king and his men. The young boy was Alexander the Great, and later, he conquered the known world of his day. What was the secret of this boy's power over the horse? He observed that the horse was frightened by the lengthening shadows cast by the late afternoon sun, so he merely turned his back to the shadows, and removed the horse's fears. Alexander's father put his arms affectionately about his son and said, "One day you will rule the world." And that prophecy proved accurate.

1. Listen to the master mind within. There is a vast Intelligence in all of nature that regulates and operates the entire universe. This Master Mind also works through your own mind; if you learn how to tap its power you will have increased your mental capacity at once at least fifty per cent.

See how this Master Mind works in nature. The maple tree produces seed that the Master Mind has given wings, like a parachute. Why wings? Because this Intelligence *knows* that if the maple seeds fall in the shade of the mother tree they will have little chance to survive, so they have wings that the wind can catch and blow to a sunny patch of ground. This Intelligence leaves nothing to chance to assure the success and perpetuity of her creation; she gives the maple tree literally thousands of winged seed, to be sure that some of them will survive the caprices of Fate.

Learn to listen to the Master Mind within. Be in tune with it; it wants your success and happiness *more than you do!* Emerson speaks of this Master Mind; William James called it the Universal Mind, Edison believed in this super-intelligence, and spoke of his Mental Brownies, who gave him most of the great ideas he had for his movie camera, the electric light, and his hundreds of other inventions. Robert Louis Stevenson spoke of this higher mind, which gave him all his stories and details which he himself did not even know. Shakespeare is believed to have used this great creative mind that is in all of us, for he was the son of a butcher, with a very limited education, and yet he wrote of royalty and court experiences in language that had such nobility and grandeur it has baffled the learned minds of all ages.

Take time out each day to sit quietly and listen to the instructions this Master Mind is trying to give you. If you have a problem go into the silence of your own mind and quietly ask this power to give you a solution to the problem. If you want to be guided to riches, ask the Master Mind within how to develop your talents, how to discover some secret, how to create some work that will bring you success and fortune. This Master Mind knows the chemistry of your body and brain; it created your entire body; it knows the secrets of the soil, the stars, the rivers and oceans. *It is* the power back of all life. Why not use this power? The next time you mislay or lose something, test this intelligence. Quietly say to yourself, "Nothing is really lost in the universe. The Master Mind *knows* where it is right this moment. I shall be still and be guided to finding the lost object." Then go about your business. You will suddenly stumble onto it, or a still, small voice will tell you where to look for it. I have known thousands of people over many years who used this secret of the Master Mind, and through it they have found lost objects, been led to the discovery of great ideas, and the evolvement of their minds to a point where they can solve problems, and meet all the challenges of life with poise and certainty.

2. Expand your thinking to encompass broader fields of experience and action. Most people limit themselves to habit-patterns of thought that include their small, every-day happenings. They never allow themselves to soar into the unlimited world of creative thought where they envision wonderful experiences, better jobs, bigger income, the accumulation of a fortune. The habit patterns of thought become chains that bind them to lives of inactivity, poverty and limitation.

Learn to *think big!* Your brain cells are aching for exercise in big thinking. Think of the limitations of thought in the lives of those people you know. Most of them are in positions where they make a limited income and they are doing nothing to change their mode of thought or life. Everyone knows how to think small, but it takes a truly expanded mind to think big.

Samuel Johnson said, "The true, strong, and sound mind is the mind that can embrace equally great things and small."

Has your mind been embracing small things too long? Try changing this, and let your mind embrace *big thoughts;* see yourself living in that new house or bigger apartment; see yourself working in the new position, making a bigger salary. See yourself doing things you want desperately to do; taking a long trip, painting, writing, singing, acting; following hobbies you enjoy. *If you do not expand your thinking to include these things* you will never do them!

3. Gather as much knowledge as you can consciously—then let your subconscious take over and use it. Most people make too much effort to do the really big things of life. They seem to feel, somehow, that they have to do the actual work. Stop and ask yourself what power it is within you that does your breathing, that digests your food, that works your mind. You will realize then that the really big things are *done for you* by your subconscious mind.

To let your subconscious work better for you, gather as much knowledge as you can consciously about the subjects you wish to become expert in, then turn over this mass of material to your subconscious and let it do the work of sorting out, storing, filing, and using the knowledge you have accumulated. *Do not try too hard to remember these things,* for effort or tension causes you to forget. Remember when you have forgotten a name, how much effort you made to recall it? Then, when your conscious mind became exhausted or discouraged and *stopped trying* the name popped right into your mind!

The facts are waiting for you. The facts are waiting for you, stored there in the amazing memory of your subconscious mind. If you keep studying to improve your mind, exercising your brain cells, expanding your consciousness, gathering knowledge and facts, you will be strengthening this faculty of the subconscious, giving it more to work on, and finally it will release all these facts and many more, new and original ones it will make up, for you to use in getting rich, finding a better job, buying the things you want, or finding solutions to your problems.

How the Beaver Uses this Power

It is the nature of a beaver to build dams across streams. This secret is an in-born thing that every beaver possesses. Scientists once took a beaver home and locked it into the living room for a few hours to see what he would do. When they came back the beaver had laboriously chopped all the furniture up into small pieces and dragged them to a corner of the room, where it had built a perfect dam for a non-existent stream! You can't stop a beaver from building a dam, no matter where you put him; it's his nature.

So too, you cannot stop this power from working for you, if you will let it, but you must give it substance with which to work, you must add to your knowledge, give it facts, then trust this power within to re-arrange the facts, assemble them into neat, orderly patterns of thought, and release them through your conscious mind as new, original and powerful ideas that can change your life.

4. Give yourself a five-year plan for mental growth. Your mind likes *definiteness*. Give yourself a five-year plan for study, growth, and evolvement. In that time promise yourself a complete new mental viewpoint, new environment, new work, new friends, a higher income and better standards of living. Your mind likes such a challenge as this. It will rise to the occasion and give you the mental power you may need to achieve your five year goal. Do not stop, however, with a five-year plan; keep expanding and changing this plan as the years go on, so you always have an unfinished symphony of life which you are working to complete. This gives added purposefulness to living. Pick the books you want to study in that five-year plan, the courses you wish to take in evening school or by correspondence, the steps you wish to take to set up a new social life; the friends you wish to cultivate. Do *more than just think these things;* write them down, make a comprehensive list of your plans and aspirations, so you can consult your list frequently and see that you are on the right path.

5. Create a need in your life for something you want. If you vaguely say, "I want more money," "I'd like to go to Europe next year," or "I'd like to get married." These statements are weak and inconclusive. Everyone thinks such thoughts once in a while. You must create a need in your life for the things you want. If you want more money, *find a need for more money*. What do you want more money for? Be specific and tell yourself what you will do with it. Why do you want to go to Europe? For fun? For cultural improvement? To meet a rich marriage partner? For relaxation and rest? Have a real need, and keep re-affirming that need, until it crystallizes in your mind as a dynamic demand on the universal life intelligence.

"Necessity is the mother of invention," it is said. Build the necessity in your life for the new home, the bigger apartment. Take the step and buy the new car, the new furniture for your home; don't worry about *how you will pay for it!* If you once take the step, create the need, the money will come to meet that need. This secret is what most of the great men and women of history have used to build power, fortune, fame. The need for more money to pay on your home or furnishings, the desire and need for that TV set you buy on time, will lead your mind to be resourceful and *find the means to pay for these things!*

6. Make your mind do some creative act each day. Nothing builds latent mental powers so much as each day making your mind do some creative act. You may not see any immediate results in these small, creative efforts, but you can take my word for it, they will gradually build giant mental power.

Victor Herbert wrote music for over forty years *without winning recognition,* but every day he sat down and courted the creative muse within, writing a little, patiently waiting and perfecting his talents. Forty years later he won his great success with *Babes in Toyland,* and established himself for all time in the light opera and musical comedy field.

You may say "I don't have time to do this, I'm too busy making a living." I say, *find time!* Each day sit down and try to think up some creative act for that day; something to help you in your home, something you can use in business, a new idea you wish to try out, an invention you bring to mind, a story you plot, even if you do not write it; the main thing is, *keep using the creative faculties of your mind until they grow strong!*

This Secret Made Her $5,000,000!

A woman had three small children to raise when her husband died. She was a nurse. She had a secret desire to become a great writer, for two reasons; one, to make money to rear her family; two, because she loved doing creative work. But she was so busy working twelve hours a night as a nurse that she never had time to work on writing, or she was so tired when she came home in the morning, that by the time she had cared for her family, packed their school lunch and saw them off, she was too exhausted to write the big stories she had in mind.

One morning she made up her mind she would write just a few words, and keep on each day until she finished a story. She sat down and wrote, and kept writing, until finally she fell asleep at the table!

But from this simple determination to keep at it, she built a mental habit that persisted for months and years; she kept writing in her spare moments at the hospital, each day when she came home from the hospital, until her first novel was written. She sent it off to a publisher. It was a success; then followed many novels, plays, short stories, until she made the astonishing sum of five million dollars! This woman's name was Mary Roberts Rinehart.

7. **When you experience defeats come back and try again.** A muscle grows by repeated exercise; a brain cell grows *only* when you keep trying, thinking, studying to develop your mind. You need persistent and daily mental exercise if you wish to build your mental power to its fullest capacity. Increase your mental capacity by repeating your efforts over and over, even in the face of seeming defeats.

When someone asked the mighty Babe Ruth of baseball fame, what he thought about when he stood on the diamond waiting for the pitcher to throw the ball, the great Babe replied, "I think of only one thing; of hitting that ball!"

Your mind must have this persistent and determined feeling about the goal you are trying to achieve. When you experience defeats, you must keep trying and trying until you are able to overcome that defeat, and achieve success.

Dynamic Action and the Cellular Theory

Science has recently learned about the Cellular Theory, the ability to imprint upon the cells of our brains and bodies *the pictures and thoughts we most persistently hold.* To do this more forcibly repeat over and over the thoughts you wish to incorporate in your mind, the suggestions you wish it to follow. Write down on little filing cards forms of dynamic action that you wish to incorporate in your thinking, knowing that through the cellular action, these thoughts will gradually be given to the nerves and muscles of your body and externalized in dynamic action.

Some of these verbs of action you might concentrate on, could be: *"I will think big." "I will be more." "I am great." "I desire riches." "I move towards my great destiny confidently." "I can achieve." "I conquer circumstances." "I build on faith." "I have supreme confidence."* These words all express dynamic action, and move your mind in the direction of positive achievement.

A Great Violinist Used this Secret

Jascha Heifitz, one of the world's greatest violinists once told me the secret of his success backstage at world-famous Carnegie Hall, when I attended one of his concerts. When I entered his dressing room, he was walking back and forth, with his million dollar Stradivarius under his chin, *practicing!* I was aghast, for it was only ten minutes before concert time.

When I asked Heifitz why he was practicing he replied, "I practice eight to ten hours a day. Before I won success in my first concert I practiced every day for that length of time for *twenty years.*"

Here was the secret of the cellular theory and dynamic action in living motion! That was the million dollar secret used by a man who has made millions of people happy, and, who, incidentally, has made several million dollars through his concerts.

8. Do not accept any limitation on your mental powers. This priceless ingredient of our Million Dollar Secret is vitally important. Many times it is not the knowledge, the talent, the greatness that a person possesses that brings him success, fame and fortune. A little talent will go a long way if a person refuses to accept limitations on his abilities.

What if you wanted to write a great novel and told a friend about your ambition, and the friend laughed at you and asked, "Who do you think you are—Shakespeare?" This might tend to discourage you and depress your creative flow of ideas, and you might give up even trying.

If you refuse to accept limitations on your mental powers and your talents, you will set to work to create according to your present mental capacity. The moment you begin, you will be astounded at the sudden flow of power and ideas that will come to you. You will then be inspired to continue your work and you will win success.

How a "Simple Housewife" Used this Million Dollar Secret

Very often people think they are limited in their ability to create greatness by their circumstances. Housewives constantly come to my lectures, and after listening to me for a few weeks, say, "How can I do these great things? I'm only a simple house-wife." There is nothing "simple" about being a housewife; they have great talent and ability, and if aimed in the right direction they can and often do achieve greatness.

Such a simple wife wrote one of the best-sellers of all time in the fiction field. Her name was Margaret Mitchell, and she wrote *Gone with the Wind*. I once interviewed this noted author, to discover her Million Dollar Secret. Here is what I learned. She wanted to be a writer, but she didn't want to disturb the even tenor of her and her husband's life, so she wrote part time, while her husband was away. She persisted for seven years with her writing of *Gone with the Wind*. Her main idea was to be doing something she enjoyed, something creative, to get her away from the hum-drum, ordinary activities of housekeeping. She was not a Shake-speare, but she did a great work, by never once limiting her cre-ative ability or listening to the discouraging remarks of her friends.

9. Organize your thinking by organizing your life. Order and harmony are God's first laws for creation. If you live in a constant state of confusion and disorder, you cannot have an orderly mind.

You can begin today to organize your thinking. You start by first organizing your life. Have a daily schedule for shopping, for your social life, for your working habits, for your housework, or what-ever you have to do daily. If you do things at regular hours, your mind will soon acquire the habit of neat and orderly thinking and will be ready to help you by releasing power to do these things in an easier manner than if you leave everything to haphazard chance.

If your mind is allowed to ramble, if it is unruly and disorgan-ized in its thinking, it will reflect in everything you do. The great-est things accomplished by great minds, have been due to their ability to organize their thinking and their environment. Set aside a certain time to study each day, and improve your mind. Have a definite time to get up in the morning, a certain time you eat your meals; regular time for exercise, for sitting down and med-itating on your problems.

Power through Great Expectations

Organize your thinking about one central theme; *great expecta-tions*. Each day tell yourself that you are going to do something great that day. Look forward to these opportunities, expect people to help you, look for chances all about you in your daily work, your home environment, where you can experience emotions, unusual events.

It is estimated that one reason why so many foreigners who migrate to this country make a success in their chosen field, is because they *have great expectations.* They literally expect to find dollar bills in the streets. This keen expectation, this eagerness on their parts to make good, leads them to take steps that bring them the success they expect.

Make it a point each day, when you start out in the morning, to tell yourself that you will discover something great that day, or that something unusual will happen to you to help you achieve your goal.

A great scientist gave credit to a manservant he had for many years, who awakened him promptly at seven each morning with this bright reminder, "Wake up, there's great work ahead today!" This reminder, this expectation of great work and achievement gave this scientist unusual impetus for his day's work.

10. Be inspired by noble emotions and high ideals. No person has ever achieved great heights who was not first inspired by noble emotions and high ideals. How can you get such high inspiration in your life? You can do it by listening to beautiful music. This often releases great creative inspiration. Music reduces fatigue, increases the flow of energy. You can read inspiring lives of great men and emulate their examples. You can read beautiful poetry or great literature. You can release the emotional power of Love in your life, so that it tends to inspire you to create greatness and beauty for the one you love.

Many Facets to a Diamond

There are many facets to a diamond; the more facets, the greater the reflective ability of the diamond, and the more it increases in value.

Your mind might be likened to a diamond; if you have few interests, few original thoughts, your mind cannot give off reflections of knowledge, truth, power; but by polishing your mind, increasing the number of facets in it, you can also increase your mental power and your ability to achieve more in life.

The more things you are interested in in life, the greater will be your mental capacity. Make it a point to acquire information on everything that is of interest to you; study the latest magazines, especially those dealing with current events, keep up with the world, show an interest in what's going on in other parts of the world, for in so doing you are adding more facets of mental interest to your brain. You will become more valuable to the world, and the world will give you richer rewards in money, recognition, fame, and satisfaction because of the new mental power you will possess.

Respond to Challenges with Action

When your mind has some challenge to meet, such as rejection, defeat, or failure in some project you attempt, instead of retiring from the scene, admitting defeat, you must respond to the challenges with mental and physical action. Toynbee's theory of the advances civilization has made is simply one called "challenge and response." Every challenge calls forth some kind of response—either one of fight or flight. If you stay and fight it through, your brain and your body grow stronger under this stimulus, and you evolve a step higher on the ladder of success.

Have you ever watched a baby chick being born? You will see how it has to summon up great strength to fight the challenge of extinction, in order to be born. It literally pecks its way out of that hard shell, completely unaided.

I remember when I first saw a baby chick being born in an incubator on the farm where I spent my early years with foster parents. All the baby chicks had been born except one little fellow that kept pecking and pecking at his shell, but he couldn't quite make it. He'd stop a while and rest, then try again, finally he lay still, with only part of his little head showing. I felt sorry for him and reached out my hand to crack the shell and make it easier, but my foster father stopped me. He said, "No, son, do not help him. Any chick that hasn't the strength to emerge from his shell alone, probably would not survive life anyway." I turned away regretfully, but I learned a great lesson in that example from nature.

Additional Pointers for Mental Power

1. Dwell on positive thoughts of success, health, happiness, riches, achievement, rather than negative thoughts of fear, failure and unhappiness. The positive thoughts tend to charge your brain, like a storage battery; whereas the negative thoughts tend to short-circuit the battery of your mind and thereby weaken and limit your mental power.

2. Have a higher incentive than one of making money; the higher your incentive, the greater will be your mental power.

3. Have enthusiasm for everything you do. Your mental power will grow under the impetus of enthusiasm. Look forward to every new experience in life, with eagerness, and soon your mind will acquire a sharp edge of enthusiasm that will make life a constant adventure.

4. Build habits of control in your thinking processes; instead of letting your thoughts run away with you, learn to say "Whoa!" when they become especially obstreperous or chaotic. A serene mind is a powerful mind, but one that is confused and agitated by every passing storm lacks power and persuasion.

5. Believe in the things you are doing, for this faith in yourself and your work, increases your mental power tremendously. Marcus Aurelius said, "In the morning when thou art sluggish at rousing thee, let this thought be present; 'I am rising to a man's work.'" When you once start your mind going with this affirmative statement, it will keep going all day with a high level of inspiration and power.

6. Summon your will power to the surface, if your mind should show signs of indolence. The hardest thing in the world is to *make people think*. If you suffer from this problem, repeat to yourself or aloud such statements as, "*I Will* myself to take action in solving this problem." "*I Will* myself to get the job I am going after." "*I Will* myself to make the extra money I need." There is power in such statements of will. A great philosopher once said, "The good or ill of man lies within his own will."

13

Building a Strong
Master Motive

What are the master motives in back of your life? If you know the dynamic urges that are driving you towards the achievement of your life goal, it may be easier to achieve your goal than if you do not know them.

Every person who has achieved anything worthwhile, whether it was a million dollar fortune, world recognition, the building of an industrial empire or even the creation of some great work of art, had a strong Master Motive.

Psychologists have discovered that the mental and physical drives we have in life are determined by the motives behind our actions. In fact, the word motive means an inner drive or impulse that causes one to act. It is also the incentive that leads one on to his goal.

The Desire to Accumulate a Fortune

The desire to accumulate a fortune is one of the most prevalent master motives in the world. It seems that everyone wants to have a million dollars. Many people will not admit this desire to have a fortune, but psychologists put money high on the list of the things that drive people to all kinds of frenzied actions. Every person who loses his money in the stock market, or through a gold-mine or oil stock swindle, generally did so because of this Master Motive to accumulate a fortune. There is nothing wrong with this

Master Motive; in fact, it is a good one, if it is tempered by balance and moderation. The Golden Midas Touch is strong in all of us, but we have to be extremely careful that the inordinate desire for gold doesn't turn into a Golden Curse!

If you feature this Master Motive in your mind, the desire to accumulate a fortune, you will undoubtedly have plenty of money in your lifetime. But with this Master Motive there must be some other drive added; what do you want a fortune for?

Desire to Help Your Family

If your answer to the above question is: "To help my family, to educate my children; to buy a better home to rear my family in," then you have tempered with wisdom your desire to accumulate a fortune. Your chances of achieving the building of a large fortune are enhanced seventy-five per cent if *you want the money for something constructive and good.*

If you answer that you want a fortune so you can have a better time, buy a bigger car, or show off your wealth to your friends, then the power of the Master Motive to accumulate a fortune is weakened and your chances of attaining a big fortune are reduced by about fifty per cent.

Greed Kills Your Master Motive

If you are greedy and selfish and want money *only* for yourself, you will kill your mental and physical drive, and probably you will never achieve that fortune you want so badly. A desire for money *is not enough!* There must be some tangible, valid reason why you want that money. Otherwise you'll be like the greedy farmer who said, "I ain't greedy. I only want all the land what joins onto mine."

You can intensify this Master Motive for a fortune by the following steps:

1. Have a reason, preferably unselfish, why you want the fortune.

2. Plan on doing things for other people with your money; helping charity, orphans, veterans' groups, prison reform, foundlings' homes, work for the blind.

3. Have a desire to raise the standards of the world with your money. See the good the Rockefeller Foundation is doing for the

world. The Ford Foundation also serves the world with its millions. Always have some big plan in mind for doing good for the world when you desire fortune.

4. Determine that you will never use your money for any destructive or degrading act. One man I heard of once wanted a fortune, and he received it through an inheritance. He drank and dissipated, and gambled. One day, while drunk, he was driving a car and hit a child, killing him instantly. This man is still in the penitentiary for his crime. The first crime was against himself, in using nature's wealth to abuse himself; his second crime, for which he is paying in prison, was against society, for the irresponsible use of his wealth as a tool of destruction and death.

The Master Motive for Great Achievement

There are many people to whom money means nothing. They are happiest when achieving something great. This can be creative work, such as writing a book, painting a picture, sculpturing in clay, composing music, or inventing something. Even if the world never gave them recognition or wealth, these creative minds would still want to go on working. This Master Motive has produced most of the artistic masterpieces of the world.

An artist, painting in his garret, if he has enough to eat and enough to pay his rent, is often satisfied, and he has enough of a Master Motive to continue creating. But if you wish to achieve greatness in your field, it is not enough for you to be so easily satisfied. You must want to share the products of your creative efforts with the world, to give your beauty, your ideas, your genius to others, so they may also enjoy your work.

When this Master Motive is elevated to this realm, it works better for you, than if you merely want to create for yourself. Almost every scientist and inventor has worked under the impetus of the Master Motive for great achievement. They worked for the sheer joy of creating something they dreamed of, and without any idea of monetary remuneration.

Desire to Improve Yourself

Almost everyone has, as a Master Motive, the desire to improve himself. It sets into motion the mental forces that lead one to the acquisition of knowledge. This must become a very strong desire,

if it is to help elevate you to the lofty mental and intellectual pinnacles you desire.

This desire to improve yourself should lead you to the cultiva-
tion of a forceful and magnetic personality. Attention should be
given to such matters as diction, perfect articulation, the devel-
opment of a better voice, with resonance and good modulation. If
you speak in a monotone, or with a nasal tone, it will pay you rich
dividends to improve your voice by a course of study with a special
teacher in that field. Many salesmen, executives, and those before
the public need strong, good, clear voices. It is time and effort well-
spent, and will help you climb to success more rapidly.

Social Recognition as an Incentive

Many people want ego recognition, and the easiest way to
achieve this is through winning social acceptance. If this is your
master motive in life, it will work to help you achieve more success in a monetary way, so that you can have a better house, a
bigger car, the good things that money can buy. But if you can
change Social Recognition to Social Betterment, it will be an even
greater master motive for achieving success.

When you wish to win recognition from the world, you are still
limiting your power to the expression of your ego, and this con-
tributes little to the world. If you can expand your master motive
to social betterment, you will achieve more, because you wish to
give more to the world.

Darwin and How He Achieved Greatness

Darwin had one overpowering desire throughout his entire life:
to evolve the knowledge of the world to a point where it would
help everyone. He sacrificed his entire life to prove the theories
of evolution, that organisms evolve from a lowly species to a higher
form of life, and to show the impact of environment upon an
organism. His work on evolution is one of the most monumental
ever done by any human being. It will pay you rich dividends to
study his theories; it can enlarge your horizons of thought to include the entire universe.

Darwin's theories did not deny the existence of a God, as many
people believe, but merely proved that the Creative Intelligence

in the universe worked under definite, scientific laws to evolve the entire creation to its present high state of evolution.

The Desire to Win Friends

A master motive that is used by many people is the desire to win friends. This is a good motive for those who wish to achieve success, but after a while, it isn't enough to show off to our friends, and we must aim higher than this if we are to achieve truly great heights.

You can utilize this master motive as a starting point; it helps your personality to strive to become popular, to be well-liked, to have other people admire and praise your efforts. It gives your ego a boost to have many friends, and it is a Master Motive for many people throughout life. To like people and have them like you is a mark of popularity and generally shows a well-balanced, integrated personality. People sense when you like them; you cannot fool people long, and if you make that effort to be out-going in your personality, and strive to perfect the qualities of affability, charm, considerateness and kindness which make one attractive to others, this Master Motive will have served its purpose in helping you achieve fulfilment socially.

Desire for Knowledge and Intellectual Power

In hundreds of the ten thousand lives of successful men that I studied to learn our Million Dollar Secret, I found that an intense desire for knowledge and intellectual power were the master motives of great geniuses. This desire for knowledge is a driving force that is as strong, if not stronger, than the desire to make a fortune.

However, this desire for knowledge and intellectual power may be merged with any or all of the Master Motives we have studied, and it will furnish new incentive and drive to goal-achievement.

"Knowledge is power," it is said, and this is true. If your mind has all facets beautifully developed, it will function more accurately and have more power than if only a few areas of your brain are developed.

Know More—Live Longer

In a scientific study of the aged, science has evolved a new word, "geriatrics," which has to do with knowledge about the processes of aging. It was found in thousands of cases examined, where people grew prematurely old, that when the brain centers had *not been fully developed,* the person grew old faster, and did *not live as long.* It was discovered that when a person's brain cells stopped developing, the body organs and cells began to disintegrate and die! This accounts for the sad fact that many men die within three to five years from the time of retiring. It is not due to age, but to the fact their *mental power* has ceased to function for creative effort, the purpose for which they were created, and nature begins the process of disintegration. If you keep your brain cells active and growing until the age of 80 and even 90, you will find your body cells and organs will have constant regeneration and re-birth. Scientists found that the body changes every one of its billions of cells every two years; so you are *never more than two years old* at any given moment. Then as the new cells are created, they absorb the vitality and creative power of the ideas you hold in consciousness. This is the Cellular Theory, which we discuss elsewhere in this book.

Love and Sex, the Greatest Master Motives of Life

Robert Browning, the poet, said, "Take away love, and our earth is a tomb."

It is admitted by scientists and psychologists that love and sex are the two greatest drives in the human psyche. Without love, one might achieve greatness, fame, and fortune, but it is all empty and meaningless without someone to share it.

All the great music, art, literature, poetry, and even industrial and scientific achievement has been inspired by the love of some man for a woman. The beautiful Taj Mahal in India, considered one of the most beautiful buildings ever created by man, was built in memory of a woman's love.

The impulse to love blossoms early in the human mind and body; the desire to propagate and have a family is natural and instinctive. A young couple should marry early, and begin to rear a family as soon as possible. This gives the greatest impetus to success and achievement. When love is the motivating force back of life, it elevates the human consciousness to lofty heights of achievement. Love can become one of the greatest of all creative forces for good, when it is properly used. Science has discovered some amazing things about love. They find that little babies, when deprived of a mother's love, die for no other apparent reason, but if they are loved, even by a stranger, for an hour or two a day, they thrive and live!

Love—the Great Healing Force

Love has been known to heal people when all other means failed. An instance in history is that of Elizabeth Barrett, who fell in love with the handsome young poet, Robert Browning. Although bedridden and seemingly incurable, Elizabeth Barrett rose from her sick bed and married the poet, then bore him a child when she was in her early forties.

She wrote of this miracle power in the lovely couplet from *Sonnets to the Portuguese:*

> The face of all the world has changed, methinks,
> Since first I heard the footsteps of thy soul.

Cultivate these Positive Emotions for Health, Happiness, Power and Success

The positive emotions generate power. They are also motivating forces. You can generate tremendous power from the following emotions. Use them freely every day of your life.

Hope	Forgiveness	Curiosity	Desire
Faith	Enthusiasm	Confidence	Peace
Charity	Optimism	Happiness	Beauty
Love	Goodness	Acquisitiveness	

Emotionalize your thoughts if you wish them to release dynamic power. Your subconscious mind releases power to carry out any action which is induced by a *strong emotion*. Every emotion that you indulge frequently and with *intensity* is capable of giving you the power implied by the emotion. Learn to depend on these positive emotions for added strength, power and motivation.

The Negative Emotions that can Destroy You

Just as the positive emotions give life, energy, and motivation towards good, so the negative emotions give off deadly and destructive vibrations. In the study of illness that is induced by the human mind, called the Science of Psychosomatic Medicine, doctors now find that much human illness can be blamed on the following negative, destructive emotions. Avoid indulging the following emotions as much as possible. We do not need fear and worry and hate, in this modern age. We must learn to live a life that is free of them if we wish to avoid their evil effects on our minds and bodies. These negative emotions short-circuit the electrical and magnetic impulses that flow from the brain to your body. Perhaps some of your illness of the past can be laid to these negative emotions, if they have been rampant in your life.

Fear	Anger	Moodiness	Miserliness
Worry	Despair	Greed	Selfishness
Hate	Discouragement	Envy	Superstition
Revenge	Disappointment	Malice	Resentment
Jealousy	Pessimism	Sadness	

Do these Things to Build a Stronger Master Motive for Success

1. *Know what you want of life.* Do you really know what it is you want? The drives that can bring you fulfilment of fame, riches, love, happiness, are set into motion most strongly *only* when you *know* what it is you are striving for.

2. Every day of your life pick some dominating thought or motivation for that day's activity. It can be any one of these things: A desire to do good for others. A desire to create beauty for the world. A desire to share your happiness. A desire to be friendly and loving. A desire to forgive those who have hurt you. Write these strong motivations on little filing cards and keep them where you can see them daily. Use one for each day, and each positive emotion until they are strong natural drives within your consciousness.

3. Sit daily and pass pictures through your mind of yourself doing things you want to do. Then emotionalize these picture-thoughts. For example, see someone bringing you a message that

you have just come into a large sum of money. Experience the joy that this thought would bring. Or picture yourself being raised to an executive position; see yourself giving orders, getting recognition from your loved ones; receiving the bigger check at the end of the week. Emotionalize the mental images of yourself being and doing *all the things you day-dream about.*

4. Write down the ten things you would do if you suddenly came into a large sum of money. Example: I would buy a new home for my family. I would educate my children and send them to college. I would help orphans and foundlings. I would help my poor relatives. I would form a foundation to help fight intolerance and war. Pick your own ideas, and put them down; including the personal things for which you want more money, such as buying a car, new clothes, taking a trip. This will help raise new energy and give you greater motivation in the direction of achievement of these desires.

5. Learn to use the love and sex drive constructively, by not dissipating this vital force without purpose. Many young people fail in life because this constructive power of love and sex is constantly dissipated without purposefulness. Love and sex drives were given to human beings for pleasure and for procreation, but if this force is used wrongly it leads to guilt, frustration and unhappiness.

6. In your search for material wealth and success, do not neglect the spiritual values of life. The desire to live a good, honest and moral life, is based on spiritual values. The desire for inner peace and contentment that comes from living under the Ten Commandments and the Golden Rule is one of man's prime motivating forces in life. Apply the spiritual precepts found in all religions to your daily life, and you will have greater power.

14

Fortune Favors the Bold

No timid, shrinking violet ever made a million dollars!

It takes bold thinking and bold action to rise to the top of the ladder of success.

One of the priceless ingredients of our million dollar secret is: *Boldness of concept* and *boldness of action*.

Perhaps in your own life, you reached some decisive moment when you had to take a bold and decisive step in the direction of your destiny, where fortune, fame and riches awaited you. Perhaps you hesitated, fearful of taking the step from which there was no return—and you lost the biggest opportunity of your entire life.

A weak, timid, indecisive approach to life breeds inertia, failure, and misery. You may fail to act because you do not have confidence in yourself, or simply, as is true in so many cases, because you feel that everything has been discovered, invented and achieved in this age of miracles. Back in 1880 a man who worked for the U.S. Patent Office wrote a letter, resigning from his job because, he said, "Everything has been invented that could possibly be conceived of by man, and I see no future to my job."

Just stop and think what amazing inventions have come since that time! The future is as full of opportunities for those who have bold concepts and take bold steps to achieve their destiny as it was in the distant past. We are only now breaking through barriers that will lead man to some of the greatest achievements the world has ever known!

Take a Bold Step Now

The arena for action is in your own mind. Here it is that you must take a bold step now for achieving victory in the future. In your thinking you must conceive the world you want to live in, the situations you want to master, the greatness you wish to achieve. To give you greater courage, if you are one of the people who constantly say there is no longer an opportunity to make a success or build a big fortune today, let me quote a statistic that will give you confidence.

Since the end of World War II, more people became millionaires than during any other fifteen year period in history.

How did these people make their millions? Because they took *bold steps towards their goals.* They dared think big and act *boldly!*

Remember this psychological truth: *fortune favors the bold.* You must believe that this is the moment in which you will begin the achievement of greatness, recognition, fame, fortune . . . whatever it is that you have written down in your private Blueprint of Destiny.

Every one of the ten thousand cases of successful men of history that I have studied, shows that this was part of their million dollar secret to wealth and achievement. They caught the ebb tide of fame and fortune, and it was able to sweep them on to glorious achievement.

> There is a tide in the affairs of men,
> Which, taken at the flood, leads on to
>   fortune;
> Omitted, all the voyage of their life
> Is bound in shallows and in miseries.
>   SHAKESPEARE

When Is Your Flood-Tide of Fortune?

Your flood-tide of fortune need not wait for some favorable moment or some propitious circumstances. You can take time by the forelock and literally create your own circumstances. It takes bold thought and bold action to bend time and circumstances to your will, and yet, all great men have done just that; forced the time in which they lived to recognize them and their advanced discoveries.

One of the most highly paid positions in the United States, next to that of the Presidency, is that of Superintendent of New York City's schools. It pays thirty-five thousand dollars a year, and is one of the choicest political appointments of city politics. When that post came vacant in recent times, no one *dared apply for it,* thinking it was such an impossible thing to try for, as it had always been one of the local plums of Tammany Hall. However, an educator in Pittsburgh read of the vacancy and had the audacity to make application for this powerful position. Everyone was shocked at his nerve. But because no one else had the *boldness* to apply for the post, the big job went to this man, *who was not even a New Yorker,* and was perhaps no better qualified for the position than many New York educators.

Why did this man win this lucrative post? *Because he was bold in concept and bold in action!*

Executives tell me that in all big organizations they have thousands of applications for the smaller-paying jobs of eight to ten thousand a year, but *few for the higher-paying jobs* in the fifteen to twenty-thousand dollar a year class. People are *afraid to try for the big positions of life.* Afraid to act and think with boldness.

The Boldness in All Nature

Boldness and audacity exist in all nature. Look about you and see how wheat germinates in the ground to become a crop. What forces it has to fight; drought, insects, weeds, birds—all these things oppose its growth, and yet it grows and survives because this pattern of bold action is within its kernels.

There is nothing so audacious and bold as the birth of a baby. What formidable odds a new-born baby has to fight! Being born was one of the most difficult things you will ever have to achieve, and yet, you did it, because you knew nothing about it. Some automatic brain took over and made it possible for you to be born. To fight life, to meet the challenges of life, takes the same type of bold and resolute action, with a complete disregard for the dangers inherent in life. Only when you have this bold concept of yourself and your future will you be able to meet the challenges of life and rise above them.

Bold Actions Led to Greatness

When Pasteur set out to discover why the wines of France fermented, ruining their multi-million-dollar-a-year business, he worked against formidable odds. Up to that time germs were completely unknown, and when Pasteur made his great discovery, people laughed at him and called him crazy. When his theories worked, people called him a genius.

But the thing that really took boldness was when Pasteur perfected his rabies vaccine, and was willing to risk it on human life. Twenty Russians had been bitten by a mad wolf, and Pasteur sent word he could save them from death if they would rush to him in Paris. The Russians arrived, and Pasteur gave them his rabies treatment, saving the lives of most of them. This took bold and aggressive action, for the atmosphere of superstition and ignorance was prevalent at that time.

When Harvey announced boldly that the blood circulated throughout the body, people called him insane.

When Marconi told the world he could send messages without the aid of wires, it took boldness and courage to force the world to believe him.

The Wright brothers had sheer audacity as their companion, when they stepped into the cockpit at Kitty Hawk, that memorable day at the turn of the century, to prove that their heavier than air machine could fly.

What bold action Ford took, when he announced his first assembly line production, and how everyone in the automotive field laughed when he announced a design for a V-eight motor. His engineers all told Ford it couldn't be done. He told them to come back when it *was done*. Six months later they cast the first motor that was in one solid block and that was a V-eight.

Millions through Boldness and Persistence

Walter Winchell was considered bold and brassy by some. Not only had he the audacity to call a spade a spade in his news reporting, but he fought his enemies and the enemies of democracy with boldness. However, his greatest work was not only in the field of reporting. Consider what he did in the field of charity. Through the Damon Runyon Fund, which Winchell created in memory of his good friend, Winchell raised millions of dollars through boldness and persistence. Not one cent of this was kept by Winchell himself, all of it being turned over for research and work on cancer cure and prevention.

The Bold Dream that Won a Million and a Half in Diamonds

A young girl brought up in an average American family, one day began to dream of having a million dollars worth of diamonds. She never really knew where the dream began, but by the time she was twelve years of age, this dream was fixed in her mind, and she grew up with the idea that some day she would have her fabulous diamonds.

She met and married a man who was wealthy, although she didn't know how wealthy at the time she fell in love with him. They went to buy an engagement ring at Tiffany's, and before they left the store he had bought her A MILLION AND A HALF DOLLARS WORTH OF DIAMONDS!

This lady now raises money for charity. Her name is Nina Anderton, and she lives in fashionable Bel Air on the West Coast, in one of the most beautiful homes, and entertains lavishly. Her diamonds are famous, but what is more important, through her bold concepts and bold actions she has raised millions for charity. When Conrad Hilton opened his Beverly Hilton hotel, he gave Mrs. Anderton the opening night for a charity ball. That one night alone she raised over one hundred thousand dollars for charity!

America Was Built by Boldness

Think of what bold action was needed by the colonists in the early days, when they declared their independence from England! The signers of the Declaration of Independence all faced hanging as traitors, if their venture failed. It succeeded, but only because they had the boldness and audacity not to retreat in the face of formidable obstacles.

What bold action it required of Abraham Lincoln to oppose the South, and go to war rather than compromise with principle!

The decisive moment faced by Winston Churchill and President Roosevelt, and the Commander of our European Forces, General Dwight D. Eisenhower, was one that turned the tide of defeat into

victory for the Allies. If they had not acted boldly in that moment
of history, the Allies might have lost the war.

He Who Hesitates Is Lost

When Napoleon stood ready to conquer England and win the
entire continent of Europe, he lost his boldness for just a little
while and that fatal decision not to invade, brought him defeat.
A young inventor, by the name of Robert Fulton, approached the
conqueror and offered him his new steam submarine, which could
have sneaked into the English Channel and sunk all the British
man-of-war ships. But Napoleon hesitated, and that moment of
hesitation spelled his defeat.

He who hesitates is lost! Never forget this lesson from history.
You must not only have bold concepts, but you must take bold
actions, and strike while the iron is hot! No opportunity is too
small to pass unnoticed. Every person is a prospective door to a
fortune.

Power in Bold Vision

A man and woman used to come to my lectures in Carnegie
Hall. They heard me say that fortune favors the bold, and listened
attentively to many of these principles that make up our Million
Dollar Secret. He was a butler and she was a maid in a wealthy
man's home in a semirural part of New Jersey.

Using the principles I teach, of bold vision and audacious actions, they both began to visualize that this home belonged to
them; they began to use it and enjoy it as if they already owned it.
They stopped worrying about not being rich or having a home of
their own. They lived as comfortably as their millionaire master;
they had as much security as he had. I told them to begin to
project the mental picture that *this was their home,* and to enjoy
it and the millionaire's wealth as much as if it were actually theirs.

They kept up this mental projection for a period of five years.
Then I lost track of them. One day I picked up a copy of the New
York Times, and read one of those astounding Cinderella stories
that hit the papers every so often. A New Jersey millionaire, a
widower, had died; he had no one to leave his fortune to, so he left
his fabulous home and estate and half a million dollars to *his*

butler and maid! I read the names and sure enough, it was the couple who had attended my lectures so often! They had already mentally claimed their estate, and through some magic power of mind, they actually inherited that which they had kept in mind for years as being theirs.

A Young Man's Million Dollar Bold Dream

What if someone came up to you suddenly and announced that he was going to build a complete giant model of New York City, with the Empire State building to tower seven and a half feet, and every window in the colossal city made of glass, and *cut out by hand!* Wouldn't you think this a bold and impossible dream?

Yet, this is exactly what young Guy Miller did after a lecture I gave in Carnegie Hall titled, *Dream, Dare and Do.* This bright-faced, handsome young man had just gotten out of the navy and he happened to wander by Carnegie Hall, and came in to see what my philosophy was all about.

When Guy Miller told me his bold dream he said, "I have faith in you, after hearing you lecture. I believe you have the dream to see what I want to do." His idea was to build a giant model of New York City that would one day be in a permanent museum in which all the major skyscrapers and other buildings of New York would be faithfully reproduced. He showed me the Chrysler Building, which was the only building he had completed, and I became enthusiastic and offered to help him in making it possible to achieve his dream.

Ten years Guy Miller has worked on his great project, and now, completed, the giant model of New York City is one hundred feet long by twenty-five feet wide. It was used as the opening attraction of the New York Coliseum, and Saks Fifth Avenue stores featured many of the buildings in their store windows.

People laughed at this young man with his bold dream; but he disregarded them and their discouragement and worked doggedly at his project, until now, completed, it has been acclaimed by artists and architects, as one of the great masterpieces in model-building of our age. Mayor Wagner of New York City, upon viewing the model of New York City, remarked that he thought Guy Miller a genius, and the late Grover Whalen called it one of the artistic triumphs of the twentieth century.

Are You Asking for Enough from Life?

Perhaps you have not been asking for enough from life? You may have been selling yourself short. Actually your gifts and talents may be worth much more than the price you are setting on yourself.

There was once a famous singer in Italy named Catarina Gabriella. At the same time Catherine of Russia was the Empress of that vast empire. One day Catarina Gabriella received a royal command from the Empress to come to the court and do a concert. The singer sent word back by the courier that her fee for singing at the Royal Court was five thousand ducats in gold, payable in advance.

Catherine of Russia was indignant at such a demand. She sent word back, "My field marshall does not receive five thousand gold ducats a year."

The famous diva sent a message to the Empress saying, "Then get your field marshall to sing for you at court." Needless to say Catarina Gabriella got her five thousand ducats in gold. Even such a bold queen as Catherine of Russia recognized and admired such audacity!

The Man Who Boldly Asked for $75,000

During World War II, Lucky Strike cigarettes needed a design for a new package. They approached one of the leading companies that does industrial design, and asked them to submit sketches from which they would select the best. The head of this firm submitted several sketches, and the head of Lucky Strike chose the one he liked best; a simple red and green circle, with the slogan, "Lucky Strike has Gone to War" for their advertising of their new package. When the head of the tobacco company asked how much he wanted for his design, he was told seventy-five thousand dollars.

The designer thought this was a very bold and high price to ask, but the head of the tobacco company paid it. Later he told the designer, "If you had asked us one hundred thousand dollars for your design we were prepared to go that high."

This designer lost twenty-five thousand dollars because he did *not think boldly enough!*

How many times in your own life have you lost out on some reward because you did not think boldly enough.

Here Are some Pointers for Acquiring the Bold-Thinking Habit

1. **Make your decision boldly and stick with it.** Make up your mind the work you want to follow, the money you want to make, the house you want to live in, the friends you want in your life, then after making this decision stick with it, do not vacillate and change from day to day. This bold decision will shape all the events of your future life.

2. **Avoid procrastination,** for this weakens your resolve. Do not keep putting off doing the things you have chosen. Start today to take the active steps to study the course you want, to acquire more knowledge about business and finances; to prepare for the round-the-world trip, to make the social contacts you choose, to move into the house you desire; to buy the new car. You need not worry too much about where the money will come from to pay for these things; commit yourself to a course of action, and you will *discover the means to pay for it.*

3. **Bold actions with bold relatives.** If your relatives discourage you, and dim your enthusiasm or kill your dreams, you must take bold actions to restrain them. Either move away from them and their influence or immunize your mind against their negative suggestions.

4. **Refuse to believe in the impossible.** The person who achieves the impossible is the one who refuses to believe in the impossible. Do not accept the limitations others place on you or your talents.

I remember when Bing Crosby made his first screen test at Paramount. I met him on the set later, and he was worried. He said everyone told him he could never become a great singer or star because he had nodules on his vocal chords. Many people suggested he have them operated on, for it gave him a peculiar, husky tone. I advised him to ignore all the advisors, and to continue to have faith in himself. Some people advised him to train his voice and take singing lessons. Crosby ignored all these negative suggestions (given in good faith), and proceeded to work with what he had. That screen test sold for two hundred and fifty thousand dollars, and Crosby went on to make a fortune that is now reputed to be in excess of twenty-five million dollars!

5. Act boldly in face of your seeming limitations. There may be limitations which you possess, which you may feel restrict and limit you and your ability to achieve success. You may feel your lack of education is a liability, and yet Shakespeare had no formal education, neither did Dickens, and they did all right. You may have been born with what you consider too big a nose, or mouth, and yet Martha Raye, and Joe E. Brown, turned these into assets; and certainly Jimmy Durante has made millions with his over-sized nose. I often remember Marie Dressler at M-G-M when I used to have lunch with her at the commissary; everyone told her at fifty she was a "has-been," and laughed when she went to Hollywood on borrowed money to become a movie actress. She went on to make a fortune and was one of our most beloved actresses of all time.

You may say, "But the movie stars have it easier and can make a fortune more readily than others." But that's just the point, they do *not* have it easier; they have a more difficult time in a highly competitive field. It is actually easier for one who wants to become a business success to achieve it, than for one to become a star. The same qualities, the same bold concept and bold action is required to be a success in your field, as it takes to succeed on the screen.

6. Have the courage of your convictions. No one else will have faith in you if you do not have faith in yourself. When you go for an interview for an important position you carry with you a thought-atmosphere of everything you have thought, and really are. If you have thoughts of defeat and inferiority in your mind they will be written in letters three feet high on your face and in the projection of your voice, and your entire personality.

Emerson said, "What you are speaks so loudly that I cannot hear what you say."

Build your mind so that it will speak of success and happiness, poise and power. Believe in yourself, have the courage of your convictions so that others will in turn reflect confidence in you and your ability.

7. Demand the best that life has to offer. Most people are always satisfied to accept second-best from life, like a suit of hand-me-down clothing. When you ask for the left-overs of life, that's all you'll get. No one is interested in giving you more than you demand. Be sure you're worth more first, then go on and demand from people and life the respect, support and recognition you desire.

A musical comedy called *Oliver!* startled Broadway in recent times with its audacity and boldness. The originator of the idea was a young playwright who now has two plays acclaimed by the critics, which are successful: *Blitz* and *Oliver!*

The story back of *Oliver!* is an inspiring one, for it points up our concept of bold action, following bold thinking. This young writer had a friend in London who was a singer, named Georgia Brown. He told her one day he wanted to do a musical for her. She told him to get some idea and work on it. He thought of *Oliver Twist* by Dickens, so he began to write the lyrics for the show. He did not know how to write music, so he just hummed his tunes. When he'd finished it he took it to Georgia Brown and she liked it. She helped him "back" it. They raised the rest of the money through another partner and finally they produced the musical in London. It played there two years and then came to Broadway where it was a smash hit.

The star, Georgia Brown, had always dreamed that one day she would have a million dollars, own a Rolls Royce and have a mink coat. Well, today she has *two* Rolls Royces, the mink coat, and her million dollars! The bold dream, or concept, has to be in the mind first; then comes the *bold action,* that brings it out into reality and makes it a success.

8. Fight for what you believe in. If you really believe in your dream, fight for it. Do not give up without a struggle, and if you are forced to give up on one dream, get yourself another one as soon as possible. Remember the words of the song from *South Pacific?* "You gotta have a dream, for if you haven't got a dream, how can a dream come true?"

9. Build your sense of self-importance and value. None of us is born with a feeling of self-importance; it is something we must build. A sense of value only comes to you when you build your mind. This process of acculturation is what we call education, but actually it is a lifetime process which must continue long after we have left school. Formal education only gives us the tools to use for learning how to live but actual knowledge comes from the process of *living*. You build your sense of self-importance by study-ing constantly; even if you have acquired the specialized knowl-edge necessary for your profession or business, you should con-tinue to build your brain power and develop your brain cells. Some people study algebra or higher mathematics for this pur-pose; others take up Latin or Greek or some other foreign lan-guage; not so much because these things will ever prove useful, but merely as mental exercise to develop all the facets of the mind, giving more power and acculturation to the entire personality.

10. Convert your wasted hours into gold. Bold actions are no good if you waste the precious stuff of life ... *time*. Think of how many wasted hours there are in the average person's life! If they could convert this wasted time into knowledge, they could become suc-cessful in half the time. Make it a point to eliminate as much of this waste of the gold of life as possible. Each day set aside an hour or more for reading self-improvement or other worthwhile books. Too much time is wasted in looking at movies or TV programs that contribute absolutely nothing to the sum total of mental power or knowledge. Some of this type of entertainment is all right, but be careful how you spend your hours; they are more precious than gold!

15

The Hidden Ingredients of
the Million Dollar Secret

Throughout this book I have given you the principles and laws of the Million Dollar Secret that Lies Hidden in Your Mind. Some of you discovered this secret in the first page or the first chapter. Others, perhaps, have not yet discovered the Million Dollar Secret, and you may be wondering why you missed it and what it is.

The Million Dollar Secret has not been put into so many words, for it's impossible to sum up a whole lifetime philosophy in a word, a phrase, or a chapter. If you have earnestly studied this book, you will have discovered the Million Dollar Secret long ago. Each word, each chapter, has been like an arrow, pointing the way to the gradual and complete unfoldment of this priceless secret that has ·changed the lives of millions of people.

You know by now that the Million Dollar Secret is *not* money nor money values alone. You would never place such a limited value on this life-secret force. Who would take even a million dollars for his health, his inner contentment and happiness, his peace of mind and soul serenity? Who would exchange his eyesight for a million? Who would give up the priceless privilege of listening to a Beethoven concerto, or hearing the laughter of our children, bird song, the voices of those we love, for many millions? Your hearing is worth more than a million.

Who would sell his conscience, his integrity, his character and debase or demean it for millions of dollars? Who would give up the joys of love and companionship and choose to live on a desert island alone, surrounded by millions of dollars worth of gold? Who would slave and work and kill himself prematurely to become a millionaire in a lonely cemetery?

Man Shall not Live by Bread Alone

If you have read and studied this book with the thought that the Million Dollar Secret was limited to the creation of material fortune alone, then you have missed the entire point of this study.

The words of James Terry White give us one of the priceless ingredients of our Million Dollar Secret.

If thou of fortune be bereft
And in thy store there be but left
Two loaves, sell one and with the dole
Buy hyacinths to feed thy soul.

The Bible says it more simply: "Man shall not live by bread alone, but by every word that proceedeth out of the mouth of God."

The following easy-to-take capsules of psychology and philosophy, will help give you the hidden ingredients of our Million Dollar Secret, and focus your mental power for the achievement of material treasures, mental gifts, or the priceless rewards of social position, friendship, love-fulfilment and inner contentment.

These Secret Ingredients Will Cause People to Give You Money and Make You Rich

1. Give something of value to the world. You want more of the material treasures of life, but are you willing to give something of value in return for them? In checking the lives of over ten thousand famous and rich men and women, I found that the value they received in money, recognition, fame, or power, was directly in proportion to *what they gave the world*. Mental energy, time, service, personality, gifts, and creative talents, are all *convertible into gold* or other things of value.

I discovered that the people who give things to the world that help the greatest number attract money easier than those who create for a small group. The scientists, inventors, and creative minds, such as writers, dramatists, actors, singers, and producers, seem to make the biggest fortunes, because they are bringing products, comforts, luxuries, entertainment and value to millions of people. Find what it is the world needs, and then set to work producing it for the greatest good of the greatest number of people and your fortune is assured.

2. Put integrity and quality into your services or products. The hidden ingredient used by many people is integrity and quality. This applies to whether you make bread or manufacture automobiles. If you want the world to proclaim you, give people these secret ingredients and they will make you rich. But this also applies to other values than monetary ones; what makes a good friend? Someone you can depend on; his honesty and integrity, his character, stamp him and his actions. This ingredient can be used for winning love and holding it also. In fact, it applies to every creative act of your life.

3. Think of new things to improve and change people's lives, and they will make you rich. It was the newness of products like nylon, plastics, wire and tape recording, TV projection, transistor batteries, frozen foods, canning foods, and all the other modern discoveries and inventions, that made them so great. Look about you, in your own work or home, and see how you could improve or change the things about you, and make it easier for people to live, or to enjoy life more. The world will reward you with recognition and money.

4. Work to add to the comfort of people, to raise their standards of living, or to improve themselves, and you will win the support and recognition of others also. People are all anxious to raise their standards of life, and if you can think of some service, or some product to help people in being more comfortable, or having higher standards of living, your fortune is made.

5. If you can add to the world's knowledge or show people how they can use their knowledge to best advantage, people will respond to you and give you money. One of the greatest advances in modern knowledge was in the formation of home correspondence courses and this has led to a complete revolution in the fields of education. Now, at home, one may complete his high school education, take a course in mechanics, electronics, hotel management, and almost any other subject. Millions of people enroll in such courses, and millions of dollars are spent for books and courses in these fields.

6. If you can show people how to be healthy and eat right, you have another sure means to a fortune. Gaylord Hauser has made

a million through lecturing and writing books on these subjects.

Elizabeth Arden has built a multi-million dollar business a year, catering to women who want to lose weight and be healthy and efficient.

Then there are those who help inspire and uplift people and who cater to a deep-seated need for soul-inspiration, peace of mind and peace of soul. Such workers are humanitarian, and their efforts deserve support and recognition.

One of the best known in such inspirational work is Dr. Norman Vincent Peale, whose books and inspired radio and TV appearances have helped millions. Another, who has made a great name for himself in helping inspire millions of people through his ministry on TV and in halls throughout America is Billy Graham, with his crusade to bring people into closer association with their churches. He has had the confidence of presidents and appeared frequently at the White House. He inspires young people to live up to the age-old principles of the Ten Commandments, the Sermon on the Mount and the Golden Rule.

7. If you can build people's egos and make them feel a sense of self-importance, you will win a fortune.

Dale Carnegie wrote a famous book on this subject and founded an institution on public speaking and self-improvement that is still making a fortune long after his death.

Josephine Dillon, who trained Clark Gable and who discovered and made Ely Culbertson famous, was such a dynamic, inspired woman. She was able to make people project their talents to the world through her technique of training.

Lee Strasberg, the noted drama coach, who is responsible for over fifty of our greatest Broadway stage and movie successes, is another such person who has a knack for bringing out the ego in another person. When the late Marilyn Monroe's will was read, it was found she left half a million dollars to this great teacher for helping and inspiring her.

These Hidden Ingredients will Cause You to Become a Leader of Men and Win Their Respect

1. Treat your co-workers and subordinates as equals, not as inferiors.
2. Raise the feeling of self-importance in others.

3. Give praise and flattery when deserved.
4. Be fair-minded, and give credit when it is due.
5. Avoid open criticism of others. Point out what is wrong quietly and when the person is alone.
6. Avoid open arguments with people.
7. Talk to others about things that interest and concern them rather than about things that interest you.
8. Do not try to force people to do things your way; make them want to do things to please you, by showing your appreciation and respect for their efforts and ideas.
9. Let the other fellow express his opinions and give suggestions, instead of adopting an I-know-it-all attitude.
10. Show people how they can better their situation in life.
11. Share your good with others; they will respond with respect, admiration and their full-hearted support.
12. Have full confidence in your co-workers.
13. Learn how to relegate authority and responsibility to your co-workers.
14. Dare to think you can become a leader of others.

These Hidden Ingredients will Make People Like You and Befriend You

1. Pay attention to other people and be sincerely interested in them and their needs.
2. Admire and respect other people's talents, possessions, and personalities.
3. Smile and show friendship to others; they will respond with friendship.
4. Be kind and courteous; people respond to kindness.
5. Talk about pleasant, happy and positive things, not about disasters, failures, accidents, death and sickness. People run from those who are crepe-hangers.
6. Try not to borrow money from friends; this is a good rule to follow for borrowing or lending.
  "Neither borrow yet, nor lend,
  If you wish to keep a friend."

In certain cases, where you've known the person for years, this rule may be relaxed, but in most cases, you will lose the money and the friend. Better never to build friendship on this unsteady basis.

7. Do not boast about your possessions, your wealth, your home, your children, for this has a tendency to make people freeze and judge you a braggart.

8. Encourage people and praise them when they turn to you for advice or guidance on their various projects.

9. Try to see the other fellow's point of view, even if you do not agree with it.

10. Let the other fellow do most of the talking, while you listen. I know one insurance salesman who outsells all his co-workers because he is a good listener to the other fellow's humorous stories.

The Hidden Ingredients that can Cause You to Become Famous and Successful

1. Dare to dream big dreams that will dazzle the world with their concepts and daring. The world is waiting to recognize your genius.

2. Have faith in your talent, your product, the services you are trying to sell the world. People sense instantly when you are lacking in this hidden ingredient. Back up your faith with positive action. Act with confidence, talk as if you really believe in what you are saying. If you are trying to sell some product you must really be convinced of its superiority yourself or you cannot put sincerity into your sales talk.

3. Enlist the aid of other people to help you. No one ever achieved success or greatness alone. This means you must judge the character of others accurately so you do not mistakenly put faith in some person who is of the wrong caliber. Many potentially great men have been ruined by their partners, but, on the other hand, many have been helped to fame and fortune by the men they associated with.

4. If you really want to make a fortune, use this hidden ingredient; give the world a product that is reasonable and which has quality. You know the saying, "If you make a better mousetrap, the world will beat a path to your door." But be sure the product you turn out is a good one, and that it is priced reasonably, so you can make a fair profit, and you will find that your product will sell. Woolworth built his fortune on this hidden ingredient; Macy's slogan is, "We will not be undersold." Quality for a smaller price has built a fortune for many businesses.

5. Dramatize your personality, to win attention. A surgeon I once knew at Mt. Sinai hospital, Dr. A. A. Berg, had a dramatic goatee, which made him look distinguished. He always wore a red carnation in the lapel of his suit. He built a reputation as one of our greatest surgeons, *not* because of his goatee or carnation, but because of his skill. However, it was difficult to forget the man because of his dramatic appearance.

Products achieve drama through their packaging. This has become one of the big things in modern merchandising. It's the way a product is presented to the public that gives it eye-appeal or lack of it.

It's the same way with your personality, your appearance; strive to achieve a dramatic effect in presenting yourself to the world; be original, without being freakish, and you will make an impact on others that will prove helpful in making you distinctive.

6. Bring your imagination into play in presenting yourself or your products to the public. Cellophane wrappings that show the product inside, have become successful in recent years. Some person who had imagination conceived of this idea. Bright colors, paintings, or photographs, sell millions of dollars worth of products that, otherwise would be drab and unappealing.

7. If you are trying to sell yourself or your products to someone, try to get the other fellow agreeing with you. Make him say "Yes" as often as possible, for this will psychologically condition him to be in a receptive and affirmative mood.

8. Get in the habit of writing letters to important people, suggesting ideas, offering your services, or calling attention to your products. Many times a letter will get through to an important executive when you could not get in to see him in person. One man I know who sold office equipment made sales that astounded his co-workers. His secret? He sent night letters to the heads of departments. In a hundred words he could give an impressive argument for giving him an appointment. A telegram *looks important!*

The Following Hidden Ingredients will Make People Respect You More and Raise Your Barometer of Self Respect

1. Think highly of yourself. Tests by psychologists taken in a grammar school showed that children who thought highly of them-

selves and who believed they were well-liked by others, actually were more popular and made better grades. Raise your opinion of yourself, if it should happen to be dragging in the dust. Remind yourself of this thought, "Others seem great to you only because you are on your knees. Rise, and you will be their equal."

2. Do not depreciate others, or call attention to their lacks and limitations. People do not like to be reminded of their shortcomings. They are only too well aware of them. If anything, pick some quality or trait in them that you can sincerely admire, and praise them for possessing that trait. They will remember praise with pleasure, but will hate you if you depreciate them or their possessions.

3. Give other people credit for being intelligent, and help them raise their own opinion of themselves. Give their egos a boost by admiring the things that are good, and passing over their weaknesses.

4. Show consideration for the feelings of others. Cultivate what psychologists call empathy, the ability to project yourself into another person's skin; to know how he feels, what he thinks, and how he will react. This is one of the great secrets of men who become great leaders. They **know** how others feel and react.

5. Avoid open criticism of people, especially in the presence of others. People will never forgive you if you cut their egos down to size, to show your superiority. Great men were always clever in never openly criticizing another person's efforts, or making disparaging remarks about their clothes, homes or personal possessions. This tendency to criticize is strong in some people and wins them open enmity.

6. There is profit in learning how to praise people and treat them with kindness and consideration. Employees that are given such fair treatment and recognition for their labor turn out to be better workers and have a higher level of energy than those who work under the fear of constant abuse from their superiors. Psychologists took tests to show the effect of praise on the blood sugar of a person's body, and it showed that praise raises the blood sugar and energy level instantly, whereas remarks that tend to deflate the ego, or discourage a person's efforts, depleted the blood of its supply of sugar and lowered the person's vitality and stamina.

7. Show high idealism in your own conduct, your speech and manners, if you wish to win for yourself the high esteem and respect of your co-workers, subordinates or superiors. Other people

tend to reflect us, like a mirror, when they come into our presence. If you demean yourself by telling off-color stories, even though others may laugh, it is at your expense of dignity and respect. If you show high idealism and conduct yourself with courtesy, tact, diplomacy, charm and consideration, others will respect you.

8. Honesty and sincerity are highly desirable qualities to have in your character, if you wish the respect of others. As someone has said, "If you keep on telling the truth long enough, people are bound to find out eventually." Stick by these standards of honesty and sincerity, even when it does not seem to be producing any positive results, for you are building character and in turn, character builds destiny.

9. Give value for value received. Most people cheat on life; they may not actually take money or things of value, but they steal time, or give less of their labor and effort by sloughing off responsibility, avoiding work, concealing their inefficiency, or in other ways cheat their employers. If you have built habits of stealing time or giving less value for what you receive than you should, you will gradually undermine your own character and weaken the respect and admiration of others.

You can Conquer Fear and Worry with these Secret Ingredients

1. How to break the habit-patterns that have made you fearful and worried in the past:

(a) Refuse to worry about anything that you cannot help or do anything about.

(b) Do not dwell at length on things you fear, for this tends to wear the furrows deeper into the convolutions of your brain.

(c) Fill your mind with thoughts of confidence and courage.

2. Realize that worry is different from normal concern and a sense of responsibility. Worry is the mental act of dwelling on your problems and doing nothing to solve them. Normal concern is in recognizing a problem exists and doing something positive and constructive to solve it.

3. Most fears are learned by human beings, as a child is born with only a fear of loud noises and falling. Change the negative

habits of thought which make you fear, by building confidence in your mind. Fear has the power to attract to us that which we fear. The Bible tells of this in the following quotation:

Job said, "For the thing which I greatly feared is come upon me, and that which I was afraid of is come unto me."

Fear magnetizes the thing we fear. A young couple were going to have a baby. They feared that their child might be hurt by a car, so they moved to a high hill, built a home, surrounded it with a wire fence, and when their child was at the crawling stage the husband went to the garage one morning to back his car out; the child crawled onto the driveway and his father ran over him. The child was killed by fear!

"We have nothing to fear but fear itself," the late Franklin D. Roosevelt said, and this is a great truth.

4. Counteract fear and worry by memorizing suitable quotations from the Bible and repeating them several times daily, until their comforting words are inscribed on your brain, obliterating the effects of fear and worry or other negative emotions.

Two excellent Biblical quotations to memorize are: The Ninety-First Psalm, and the Twenty-Third Psalm. Also, the Lord's Prayer.

5. To conquer fear and worry completely strive to overcome any remnants of superstition and ignorance which form a mental climate in which fear and worry thrive. Many times these negative thoughts are planted in the mind when we are children; to be afraid of policemen, to fear the bogey man, to suspect people who are of a different color from us, or who speak with a foreign accent.

6. Study the lives of great men and women, and see how they have overcome their fears and worries and triumphed over seemingly insurmountable obstacles. The lives of the two Roosevelts, Franklin Delano, and Teddy, who both overcame tremendous odds in their struggle for health, are worthy of study. Churchill's life is a monumental example of courage in the face of what seemed to be sure defeat.

7. Rationalize or reason out the things you fear or worry about by writing them down, and examining them coldly. It helps dissipate your fears if you do this, for it brings them out in the open. Then write down as many alternatives and courses of action as possible, and follow the best for solving your problems and dissipating your fears.

These Secret Ingredients can Help You Arouse Love in Another Person

1. Project love to another person and he will feel it at once, for love has about it a magnetism that arouses an emotional response in the person we direct it towards. Emerson's rule for winning and holding love is still one of the best:

Love, and you shall be loved; for love is as mathematically just as the two sides of an algebraic equation.

2. Show those you wish to love and have loved you, kindness and consideration. People respond to a show of kindness. Notice them, praise them, arouse their emotions by sharing your smiles, your happy experiences, your ideals and dreams, and they will inevitably respond to you with love.

3. Share your good with those you love, be generous and lavish your gifts upon them, without thought of what you will get in return.

4. Sacrifice something you hold dear for the one you love. It makes people feel they are something very special if you sacrifice your time, your talents, your goods, for them.

5. Recognize the good qualities of those you want to love you and give them credit for possessing these qualities.

6. Tell those you love how you appreciate them and what they are doing for you; how you cherish their love and friendship. People show too little appreciation, and thus shut themselves out of the warm circle of love which others would like to bestow on them.

7. Be polite, courteous, gentle and forgiving; these are the four absolute *musts* of love. No one loves a discourteous boor; a person who hurts others' feelings, or who holds a grudge and does not forgive, is generally not worthy of love.

8. You must be able to overlook the shortcomings and weaknesses of those you want to love, for everyone has these human weaknesses. The thing that makes most marriages fail is that we idealize the loved one too much and place him on a pedestal; then when we find he has human weaknesses we somehow resent those weaknesses.

9. Give freedom to the person you love. This is a rule that most marriage partners must learn. If you don't trust your mate, then you have no basis for a happy marriage.

10. If you feel jealousy or suspicion of the one you love, conceal it by all means, for this emotion of jealousy will help kill love.

Peace of Mind and Deep Soul-Contentment can Be Yours If You Apply the Following Hidden Ingredients of Our Million Dollar Secret

1. Learn to withdraw from the outer world of confusion, discord and friction, at least one hour a day, where you are completely alone with your thoughts. Direct your thinking to high and lofty planes of thought; ask yourself: What is the purpose of life? What is the mystery of life? What is the nature of God? Where are you going in life? These thoughts will tend to give you a sense of the universal values that exist, and make your small, petty problems and fears and worries, fade away into insignificance.

2. Implement your faith in a higher power than man or man's mind. To believe in a God is psychologically sound and healthy. Atheists are seldom happy people. An atheist once said, "I'm an atheist, thank God!" It's difficult to conceive the miracle of life without admitting of a Creator.

3. Overcome feelings of guilt, shame, and conscience pangs over what has happened in the past, by prayer, and asking God's forgiveness for the error of your ways. Then attempt to change your mode of life, and you will feel a sense of being purged of your past mistakes and so-called sins.

4. Peace of mind comes when you release yourself from living too much in the physical senses. Do not live in a world of material values alone, but seek the companionship of good books, great art and inspiring music.

5. Strive to elevate your standards of living, and enthrone the ideals of Beauty, Goodness, Love, Honesty, Forgiveness, Mercy, Compassion, Charity, and Hope in your thinking.

6. Study the nine great revealed religions of the world, and search for the unifying elements in each of them. They all stress the golden rule and loving one another.

7. Be aware that you are not just an ordinary human being; you are a child of the living God. In the first chapter of Genesis you are told, "Let us make man in our image. . ." Spiritually you are a reflection of God; therefore act in such a way that you show yourself worthy to be called a son of God.

8. Let love be the universal emotion that removes prejudice, intolerance, bigotry and division amongst people. Show love in your daily contacts with others, for love is a spiritual quality.

16

Become a Receiving Station for Great Ideas

Everything we see in the outer world is crystallized thought, mental energy frozen into matter. Science now knows that what looks like solid matter is, in reality, a vibrating mass of atoms, that are in constant motion. The form they take seems to depend on some creative pattern that is one of the secrets of the universe.

A French scientist studied frozen snow flakes for a period of forty years to learn something of this secret of form and pattern that create the universe, and he learned an astonishing thing: No two snowflakes he looked at in that forty year period were ever alike! No leaf, no fern, no grains of sand are ever alike.

The rose carries within its seed the image and likeness of all the roses that will ever be created from that seed.

The acorn has hidden in its mysterious depths all the giant oak trees that will ever be created by the earth.

The vibration that makes each form complete is a universal intelligence that is constantly shaping and creating in the invisible universe, according to some secret pattern that nature has locked up in her vast storehouse of wisdom.

As Above, so Below

There is a saying in philosophy, "As above, so below." This means that the microcosm, man, reflects all the processes and creative principles that exist in the macrocosm, or the larger universe.

Microcosm relates to an organism, regarded as a world in miniature. Man is actually a world in miniature, and he reflects in all his mental and physical processes, all the universal processes of growth, attraction, reproduction, and refinement. The seedling of reality is in man's own mind; his mind is the place where he creates the world in which he lives.

When you once understand this principle, you will know that part of the Million Dollar Secret that lies hidden in your mind exists in the **creative** power that every person has locked within his own human consciousness.

There is a picture or pattern within your mind, which has its counterpart in the Universal Intelligence; the same intelligence that creates the rose and the oak tree. There is only one major difference between the use of this Creative Power within your mind and that in nature: You, being a creature of volition and choice, may *choose the pictures you wish to create in the outer world,* whereas the animals, birds, insects, and growing organisms in nature are *forced to create according to a set pattern.*

What Is this Creative Mind?

This Creative Mind within man has been called various things by philosophers, psychologists and mystics of all ages. Jung and Freud referred to the human psyche as being the repository for all of mankind's racial memories and wisdom. What one man has thought, or experienced, or done, may be the common property of all creative minds. You can reflect the knowledge of all the great minds that have existed since the beginning of time. Just as all chicks within the hen's egg know how to peck their way out of the shell, so too, your Creative Intelligence knows how to work out all your problems, knows how to give you the ideas and inspiration to make all your dreams come true.

You can become a receiving station for great ideas, just as the famous men of history did. You can unlock the creative power of this higher mind within you, just as Napoleon did, as Michelangelo did in his creative masterpieces of marble and canvas. The power that was used by Lincoln, Columbus, Newton, Galileo, Edison, Washington, and Benjamin Franklin, is a part of your own higher consciousness. You may tap that creative mind within and receive from it all the inspiration you need to build your future destiny in the pattern of greatness and genius.

The Divine Flame within

When Moses used this creative power, he spoke of having heard a voice speak to him from a flaming bush. He was given the Ten Commandments, and shown how to lead the Lost Tribes out of the desert to freedom. When asked who had given him this information he replied, "I Am has sent me." Undoubtedly, this *I Am* refers to the Divine Flame of Creative Intelligence that is in every living human being. You may turn to this higher mind and receive the information you need to lead you out of the barren desert places of your life into productive fields of action and creativity.

The Divine Flame of inspiration works through your higher mind and can accurately point out the direction you are to take for achieving *anything you desire in life!* There are rules that must be followed, however, for this Universal Intelligence works under definite laws. William James called this transcendental power within man's mind, the Superconscious Mind. Emerson spoke of this intelligence in nature, and often referred to it as the Universal Mind. He speaks of this mystery, which encompasses all of nature and to which man may attune himself, in these words:

> The rounded world is fair to see,
> Nine times folded in mystery;
> Though baffled seers cannot impart
> The secret of its laboring heart,
> Throb thine own with Nature's throbbing breast,
> And all is clear from east to west.
> Spirit that lurks each form within,
> Beckons to spirit of its kin;
> Self-kindled, every atom glows,
> And hints the future which it owes.

When your mind is in tune with the Universal Mind that underlies all of nature and which flows throughout all creation, you are able to discern the secrets of the universe and use this creative power for any constructive purpose.

Picture and Project Your Desires

Your mind has a tremendous electrical power that is able to reproduce accurately all the thoughts, feeling, sensations, sights, sounds, and other stimuli from the outer world. Think of the miracle of the eye alone. The brain works in amazing co-ordination with this organ of vision. You do not see with the eye, but with the brain. The brain can picture and project the vibratory pattern of anything you wish to create. An artist starts with a blank canvas and what does he do? He consults the higher mind within for the image or concept he wishes to project and paint upon that canvas. The electrical pulsations of your mind are forms of creative energy; they have the power to create in the outer world of matter *anything that you accurately picture in the inner world of mind!*

Scientists have discovered, since the splitting of the atom, that tremendous power can be produced when we are able to tap the invisible wave-lengths of energy in the universe. Mohammed first discerned this secret power when he remarked, "Split an atom and at its heart you will find a sun."

The human mind is in reality a tremendous atom-splitting cyclotron, for it is able to release a stream of dynamic, creative energy and imprint upon the mould of the universal intelligence the pictures it holds within, and make them a glowing, outer reality. A rainbow has as much reality as a skyscraper; an idea, held in mind, has the ability to attract to itself all the elements it requires to build for you whatever it is you want in life.

The Great Law of Attraction and Repulsion

There are vast electro-magnetic forces in existence in the universe, which scientists have discovered since sending space ships out into the illimitable void of time and space. These electro-magnetic forces work under the law of attraction and repulsion, the law that controls the gravitational force of earth, sun and stars. This same electro-magnetic force exists in the human mind, for the mind works under similar laws as those that control magnetism and electricity. In fact, the blood is mainly saline solution, for this is the greatest conductor of electricity. What intelligence devised this amazing system of sending *nerve currents* from the brain to all parts of the body instantaneously?

This same intelligence is able to tap some mysterious power in the universe and produce that which is pictured or held in man's mind.

Great Men All Used this Power

Again Emerson speaks of this great universal wisdom that all geniuses have tapped, in these words:

Raphael paints wisdom; Handel sings it. Phidias carves it, Shakespeare writes it, Wren builds it, Columbus sails it, Luther preaches it, Washington arms it, Watt mechanizes it.

You too can become a receiving station for the great ideas that have inspired great men of all ages. The electrical law of magnetic attraction has the power to bring you that which you focus in your mind *clearly and in detail,* just as the artist forms his picture first in his mind.

Alexander the Great pictured that one day he would conquer the world, and he did.

Michelangelo pictured the great sculptures that have made him famous and which are in the great museums of the world today. This tremendous creative power does not stop working for us. Even when we are old we can continue using it. When Michelangelo was seventy-eight, he was called out of retirement to decorate the Sistine Chapel of the Vatican in Rome. He worked for four years creating the magnificent figures on the walls; over two hundred figures in giant proportions, and no two alike! He lay on his back on a scaffold seventy-five feet high, painting his concept of God's creation of Adam and Eve and the entire universe. In one scene the artist depicts God reaching out from heaven and touching the finger of Adam, inspiring man with the creative spark of life. This is truly a great symbol, and shows that when man is touched by the Finger of God, he literally becomes inspired and God-like in his concepts and the stupendousness of his creative power.

The philosopher Epictetus said of this higher mind,

When you have shut your doors, and darkened your room, remember never to say that you are alone, for you are not alone; but God is within, and your genius is within . . . and what need have they of light to see what you are doing?

The Bible also speaks of this power within, which knows all, sees all, and is all-powerful and wise. Jesus spoke of this power as the one that did His great miracles. He said, "It is not I, but the Father within; he doeth the work."

Use this Method to Become a Receiving Station for Great Ideas

1. Each night, upon retiring, spend a few moments picturing in your mind's eye the things you want to achieve, the things you wish to attract, the qualities and talents you want for your own, and even the people you want in your life. Feel that these things are already in existence awaiting your joyous discovery.

2. Ask the "Father Within" to point out the way to your right work, to the finding or making of the money you need to pay your debts; to the knowledge you need to get you a better salary; to the finding of lost or hidden objects. As this power is all-powerful, omniscient, omnipotent, and omnipresent, it works for all alike. It works to feed the birds of the air, and the Bible says of its provision for the lilies of the field, "Consider the lilies of the field; they toil not, neither do they spin, and yet Solomon in all his glory was not arrayed like one of these."

Dr. Rhine and Extra Sensory Perception

Dr. Rhine tells in his book on Extra Sensory Perception of how a girl, whose father had died, needed money desperately, as he had left her with nothing. She dreamed one night that her father came to her and told her to look in a secret compartment of an antique dresser in the living room. The girl awakened and thought it a strange dream, but, it was so realistic that she went to look for the secret compartment. She found it, and stuffed in it were many big bills, which her father had evidently saved for just such an emergency.

How was this knowledge conveyed to this girl? Through mental telepathy? Spiritism? Vibration? Science cannot explain this strange phenomena, but they know something is at work in another dimension of the universe, which seems to represent a higher mind, a spiritual something, akin to the soul, that works for man, and guides him in his time of need.

Put your problems to this higher mind within, ask for a solution, then quietly go to sleep, confident the answer will come to you, either in your sleep, or the next day when you awaken.

The In-Dwelling Father

3. If you wish to pick up thoughts of greatness, such as those that inspired the geniuses of the past, sit quietly in your room alone, and meditate on the great person whose inspiration you wish to contact. If it is Beethoven, hold his name in your mind; acquire as much knowledge as you can of his life; be conversant with his great music; then sit and wait for the highest inspiration to come through to you. Many musicians are able to produce great music by this method of artificially inducing the inspiration of the great composers of the past.

If it is a scientific discovery or formula that you want, or an invention, or business success, hold in mind the thought of an outstanding man in the field you have chosen. Then let your mind ask of the in-dwelling father that you be given the same identical ability and inspiration as that which motivated the genius you have picked.

4. You can convey messages to other persons through this process of speaking to the higher mind within you. Tell this higher mind what it is you want to convey; hold the name and face of the person in mind, then talk to them as you would if they were there in person. Thoughts, being electrical, will eventually hit the higher mind of that person, making him receptive to your projected thoughts. When you receive such thoughts, you may think they are your own thoughts, but actually, they could be the projected thoughts of another person. It is no more mysterious than the process of transmitting messages by wireless; it is the same principle involved, as both are concerned with the creation and projection of electrical impulses.

How She Got a Raise in Salary

A young lady who came to our lectures learned of this method for projecting her thoughts, and she told me she wanted to imprint on her boss' mind the thought she deserved a raise in salary.

Every day at lunch time she sat for a few moments concentrating on her boss' face and saying over and over to herself, "You will give me a ten dollar a week raise in salary." She thought this intently, she visualized him doing it, she felt the emotion of joy at the fulfilment of it, and she kept up her actions every day for two full months before she got results.

One day her boss called her into his office suddenly and blurted out, "I don't know why I'm doing this, but I'm going to give you a ten dollar raise."

Mental Messages from Other People

5. You can also receive mental messages from others through this same process of concentration and visualization. Hold in mind the face of the person you wish to receive messages from; concentrate your mind on that person for a while, and then sit perfectly still and wait and see what thoughts come into your mind. Sometimes the person will begin to speak to you mentally, and you may actually think you are imagining these things, but very often you will find that the person has actually sent out some such thoughts to you at some time.

A young lady, Dr. Rhine tells about, went on a train trip to San Francisco, and when she got off, she kept seeing the face of her mother clearly before her eyes. She became alarmed and rushed in and telephoned her home. Her mother had been sending frantic thoughts to her to tell her to return immediately, as her father was seriously ill!

6. Many times your mind will receive an inspiration to do something through an impulse that keeps returning and will not go away. This may come in the form of a vision or picture, or a thought that persists in returning, unbidden, to your mind. At such times follow through on your "hunch" for it may be some direct guidance that can guide you to fulfilment of some dream you have.

This Man Attracted a Home through this Power

An instance of this type of persistent thought was that of a young man who owned a restaurant in an eastern city. He drove by a beautiful home on the outskirts of the city one day, and something made him stop the car and sit and stare at the home. Then a thought came to him, "I would like to own that house." He felt an insistent urge that he would one day live in it, but he dismissed it from his mind as sheer nonsense, for it was a big home, obviously beyond his limited means. He had a wife and small child and his restaurant barely gave them a good living.

But he found himself driving by the house every day, and he

would stop and examine the house carefully, dreaming of it as being his. He kept this up for several weeks, when one day he noticed a middle-aged, gray-haired lady sitting in his restaurant looking at him strangely. Finally she spoke to him. She said, "I've been observing you driving by my house every day for weeks, and finally I became curious as to your purpose in doing this. I took your license number and checked on your address; that is how I found you. Now what in the world are you up to?" she asked.

The young man told her of his fixation about the house. "It's obvious," he said, "that it's way beyond what I can afford, but it's just the type of dream house I've always wanted."

Then the lady said, "It's a strange thing, but my husband died recently. The house is too big for me, as I am alone. I have long wanted to sell it. Now, what can you afford to pay down on it?"

The young man mentioned a ridiculously small sum, and the woman told him she would accept it. The purchase price she set on the house was reasonable, and they concluded a deal that gave him possession of the house and furnishings within one month!

The Formula for Receiving Great Ideas. Think . . . Visualize . . . Feel . . . Act

The whole universe teems with action; from the tiniest microscopic life in the soil to the higher organism, Man. All creation vibrates and pulsates to a higher command from some form of intelligence. Your mind is such a commanding power and it can set into motion the vibratory forms in the universe, creating the picture of the things you want to attract.

The formula for doing this is a very simple one:

Think first. What shall you think? Think inspired thoughts. Think creatively. Think dynamically. Think big. Think rich thoughts. Think successful thoughts. Think healthy thoughts. Thinking sets into motion the electrical pulsations which start the universal action necessary to create in the pattern of what you think.

Visualize. Visualize what? Visualize great things. Visualize achievement, perfection, the situations in which you wish to be; friends, love, a home, a car; more money. Hold a mental and visual image of these things so creative intelligence within you may crystallize and project these images to the outer world of reality.

Feel or *Emotionalize* your thoughts. Feel how? Feel expansive and powerful. Feel healthy and strong. Feel rich and successful. Feel confident and poised. Emotionalize your dreams and ideas, by feeling how it would be if you achieved the things you dream of attaining.

Act, the dynamic universal law of Action.

Act, how? Act with confidence, decisiveness. Be aggressive and have boldness in your actions. Play the part you wish to be on the stage of life. Are you holding in consciousness a picture of yourself as a hero or a villain? A prince or a pauper? Make your own decision as to what you want to be, but set into motion the universal law of *Action* by taking that first step here and now to make your dreams come true.

In formulating your plans for future courses of dynamic action, check first your Assets and Liabilities. In this way you will know better how to correct the things that are wrong with you, and which may be keeping you from attaining your objective.

Look over the following lists of Assets and Liabilities, and write on a sheet of paper what your own may be from this list. Also add others that may not be on this list. Then carefully appraise them, and work to correct your Liabilities, and change them into Assets.

Check Your Assets and Your Liabilities

Make out two lists, similar to the following, and head one, "Assets" and the other "Liabilities." Under Assets list all the things in your favor, such as those given in this list. Then under Liabilities list all the things that you feel you do wrong, such as those given below. Then study the two lists, and correct your weaknesses or liabilities, and strengthen your Assets.

Be honest in appraising yourself. Then, when you see your faults in black and white, it will be an incentive to do something constructive about changing them into strength of character.

Are these Your Assets?

1. I am ambitious and eager to succeed and strive constantly to achieve my high goal in life.
2. I have some ability and am working to elevate my mind by acquiring knowledge that will prove helpful in the future.

3. I am determined and persistent, and do not give up easily.
4. I never allow discouragement to get hold of me and make me moody and depressed for long periods of time.
5. I refuse to believe anything is impossible to achieve.
6. I have vision and foresight and I use it daily.
7. I constantly strive to use my imagination in trying to see my way clear to future constructive actions.
8. I do not waste my time and energy worrying about things, but I do something constructive about solving my problems.
9. I refuse to waste my time on useless pursuits that lead to nowhere.
10. I conserve my money and handle it wisely.
11. I control my temper in situations where arguments or disagreements arise.
12. I fight bad habits, including procrastination, laziness, and over-indulgence in smoking, drinking and eating.
13. I am friendly and helpful to everyone I meet.
14. I possess a strong will and never allow others to impose their will on me to achieve their selfish purposes.
15. I am generous in all my dealings with others.
16. I apply the Golden Rule to my life. "Do unto others as you would have others do unto you."
17. I live under the highest standards morally, ethically, socially, physically and spiritually.
18. I give full value for everything I receive from life.
19. My life is neat and orderly, and I am as efficient as possible.
20. I am fair and honest in my dealings with all people.
21. I do not hold grudges, or indulge negative emotions of hate, revenge, jealousy, greed, envy, or selfishness.
22. I use the emotion of love constructively in relation to the world.
23. I am punctual and on time when I make appointments.

Are these Your Liabilities?

1. I am inclined to procrastinate and put things off.
2. I am afraid of important people and limit my contacts to those who are inferior or unimportant.
3. I do not have great ability and do nothing to improve myself.
4. I am weak and vacillating in my personality and cannot make decisions easily.
5. I am easily discouraged, pessimistic and lack faith in myself and my future.
6. My personality is inadequate, self-conscious and inferior and I make no effort to change it.
7. I spend my spare time on movies, TV, sports, and having a good time, and do nothing to improve myself.
8. I seldom read constructive books or magazines.
9. I get moody and depressed often and feel that nothing I do is of any use in changing my life.
10. I feel my background and my lack of education are holding me back in life.
11. I do not use my imagination to visualize a new future for myself.
12. I am a worry-bird and do nothing to solve my problems.
13. I borrow money and get in debt, and can't pay it back.
14. I am always late for appointments and keep people waiting.
15. I believe in getting the best of people before they get the best of me.
16. I believe the world owes me a living and I don't have to make any effort to earn it.
17. I constantly blow up and have fits of temper over little things that annoy me.
18. I am negative in my thinking and indulge such thoughts as fear, worry, hate, jealousy, envy and greed, daily.
19. I am disorderly and live in a confused, chaotic and dirty environment. I do nothing to change it for the better.
20. I dislike people intensely and believe they're out to get the best of me.
21. I believe in the philosophy of "Dog eat dog."
22. I gamble and dissipate my money, time and energy.

23. I use the love force as a sexual outlet and overdo on the physical and emotional planes.
24. I let my bad habits dominate my mind and body.
25. I am weak-willed and easily dominated by others.
26. I look for ways of getting the best of everyone I meet.

When you have finished making out your own lists of your Assets and your Liabilities, set to work constructively each day to make changes in your way of thinking and living. Take such an inventory of yourself every six months to see how you have progressed. Then keep on with this self-improvement regime until you have overcome all the negative habits that put you and your life on the debit side of the ledger.

17

How to Seek and Win the Aid
of Important People

You've heard the saying, "Nothing succeeds
like success." Also, "Money seeks out money." It is true, if you
wish to win fame and fortune, you can seldom do it on your own.
You must seek out the aid of wealthy and important people.

The Quaker father advised his daughter, "Marry thee not for
money, but go thee where money is."

The working of the law of proximity is influential in the lives
of many people who have achieved success in their chosen profession. It isn't so much *what* they know, as *whom* they know. This
has become a cliche in American business, but it is nevertheless
true.

In our application of the Million Dollar Secret, let us not lose
sight of the fact that few of our great geniuses in history could
possibly have succeeded without the aid of other people.

Edison was a great inventor, but his inventions would have been
worthless to the world if they *had not been marketed*. Ford had a
great idea in building his horseless carriage, but he needed capital
and backing before he could mass produce his motor car.

Raphael and Michelangelo created great masterpieces in art,
but they needed their reigning princes of state and church and
the aid of influential, wealthy men and women, to give them the
means to achieve their great works of art.

Columbus, with his radical ideas that the earth was round could
never have undertaken more than a short journey in a rowboat if

it hadn't been for his ability to sway and win the enthusiastic support of Queen Isabella. Schwab would have been nothing without the reflection of the genius of Carnegie. The late President Roosevelt would have remained unknown if it hadn't been for the backing of Jim Farley, who entered him in the Democratic nomination for the presidency.

Greatness through Reflection

It is said, "A man is known by the company he keeps." Most people achieve greatness through reflection. It is just as easy in life to choose the company of friends who are important, influential, politically powerful, creatively active, and wealthy, as it is to associate with people who are shabby, disorderly in their thinking, lazy, disreputable, shiftless, and negative.

It has been found by psychologists that sixty-five per cent of all people who had a college education succeed in achieving their life goal. Why is this true? *Not because of their superior intelligence!* But because they were able to form friendships with men and women in college who later formed valuable links in their careers with wealthy and important families! This is the secret value of having been lucky enough to have a college education.

But if you have not been fortunate enough to have a college education, or even a high school education, does this mean that you must go through life doomed to failure?

Not at all! You have the same mind, the same personality, the same magnetism as these college-educated people. It will be more difficult for you, perhaps, but if you follow the suggestions given below, you can begin today to seek and win the aid of important people who can help you achieve your life-goal.

How to Select the Right Friends

It is important, in building your future career, to choose friends who are striving for the same goals as yourself; or people who *have already achieved these goals.* It is just as easy to form friendships with those who are going places, as to select those who are doomed by their negative habits to failure.

"Hitch your wagon to a star" is a saying that applies to the forming of friendships. Every person you admit into your life on a close, personal basis, should measure up to certain standards.

Ask yourself:

"Will our friendship be mutually good?"
"What have I to offer this person, and what has he to give?"
"Does he have habits that are negative that might impede my course in life?"
"Are his standards high?"
"Have I anything to learn from my association with this friend?"

It is not selfish for you to be concerned about these new associations, for if you see a person over three times, he has the power to change your life! You want to be sure that, given such tremendous power, these new friends will change your life for the better.

What You should Expect of New Friends

You should give certain values to your new friends, such as consideration, courtesy, help in achieving their goals, kindness, and hospitality. What should you expect of new friends?

They should add to your mental treasures and give you inspiration and incentive to achieve your goal. They should give you encouragement and constructive advice, when you need it. They should share their enthusiasm and confidences, and give you of their mental and intellectual treasures.

A new friend should have a consciousness that encompasses broad fields of action. He should bring to your friendship the qualities of vision and imagination; of courage and beauty; of tolerance and understanding, compassion and love. This is what friendship should mean in its ultimate sense.

Plan Your Social Life Carefully

A life that is planned and organized in all its details is generally an orderly, harmonious and successful life. So many people plan every detail of their lives carefully and yet completely ignore their social lives. They let this fall into a haphazard pattern that is often completely out of keeping with other orderly aspects of their lives.

More business is done over cocktails and on the golf courses than in offices, it is said. It is true that very often, important, busy executives snatch these opportunities of relaxation and conviviality to discuss business matters and make important decisions running into millions of dollars at such times.

Take advantage of this psychological fact. It is easier after a businessman has had a few drinks and eaten a good meal, to get his attention, than it is to go to his office and get through a retinue of assistants and secretaries.

I recall two meetings with noted authors that came about in such relaxed surroundings in my own career. One was the great humorist, Irvin Cobb, who was guest of honor at a luncheon I attended. The other was Rupert Hughes, a great American writer, whom I met at a party. Because he was slightly deaf and wore a hearing aid, many people found it difficult to talk to the noted author. I made it a special point to speak distinctly and loudly when addressing him, keeping my face turned towards him so he could read my lips. I spent an instructive and pleasant hour in his company, and when the evening was over, he invited me to lunch, and at another time, to play golf with him at the Lakeside Country Club near Hollywood. At the club that day alone, Mr. Hughes introduced me to some of the biggest directors, producers and stars, who later helped my career immeasurably. I was then in my early twenties, and such contacts would *have been impossible without the aid of a well-known and important person.*

Importance of Entertaining

It is important that you build your career on some social entertaining. You cannot accept invitations from others forever without eventually reciprocating. Make it a point to have small, informal groups in for cocktails occasionally, choosing key people in your business or related social groups, where you can gradually expand and enlarge your contacts.

You do not need a lavish home or apartment; some of the most charming parties I have been to, have been in small apartments. The very fact it is crowded gives a feeling of intimacy and informality that adds to the gregariousness of the event. Remember, people *like people!* Throw them together with a little food and drink, and conversation, and they will entertain themselves.

If you take businessmen to lunch, choose the key men in organizations that you believe will be useful to you in the future. Do not be afraid to *ask important people* to parties, luncheons, or dinners. Sometimes the biggest and most important people are lonely, for everyone feels they are so important that they must be extremely popular. This is not always true, and I have known many influential and important people who actually were grateful for an invitation!

Join the Right Clubs and Civic Groups

You can enormously expand your social life and get in with the country's most important people by joining the right clubs and civic groups. There are Lion's Clubs, the Kiwanis Groups, Rotary and Chamber of Commerce Groups in all communities. Make it a point to get into at least one of these. It is a foundation upon which you can build your entire social and future business life.

People who are in the professional world, such as doctors, lawyers, teachers, dentists, and optometrists, especially need such contacts with a large social group. Their business expands and grows through a process of social reference. We generally go to a doctor or lawyer because some friend recommended him.

This Man got Rich through this Principle

Salesmen, stock brokers and real estate dealers need such an ever-expanding social group for their growth and expansion in business. I remember once in Los Angeles, a young real estate salesman asked my advice on how he might expand his business and social contacts. I told him to join the Beverly Hills Hotel swimming club, where some of the richest and most successful men and women spend a great deal of their time the year around.

He joined the club, and sat in his cabana, facing the pool, invited people to lunch, and soon he was meeting the elite of the Beverly Hills and Bel Air social set. This young man was soon selling more real estate than three other salesmen in his organization. In two years' time he had his own office and his own salesmen. In five years' time he has built one of the biggest real estate businesses on the West Coast.

Big Money from Important Contacts

A jewelry salesman sought out important social contacts in New York City, and soon had built a hundred-thousand-dollar-a-year business.

An interior decorator, whose name is known from coast to coast, built his entire business success on social contacts with leading society people. He was once a famous movie star and upon retiring from the screen, took up decorating as a hobby. He has made millions. His name is William Haines.

Another man I once knew was an excellent portrait painter. He made little money until I advised him to give an exhibition of his art at a gallery in New York City and invite a selected list of important business and social leaders to cocktails at the exhibit. Soon this artist had commissions from leading society and business leaders, and eventually did a portrait of President Truman, which hung in the White House and brought him more commissions for as high as five thousand dollars each!

The sky's the limit when you catch onto the coattails of some person who is soaring to the heights. You can bask in their reflected glory, avail yourself of their important contacts, until you have gained the momentum to sail along under your own power.

A noted dress designer in Paris used this technique of cultivating important people, and is now one of the rages of the Paris fashion scene.

Use these Million Dollar Secrets for Winning the Aid of Important People

1. Offer your services and aid to civic betterment groups in your community. Here you will meet people who are in key positions and who can help you immeasurably in achieving your goal.

2. Become affiliated with your local political groups, for they have prestige and power. Many a man has started as a lowly assistant in a political ward, and risen to a position of power and prominence. You can meet lawyers, judges, and those who are big in politics, and through their aid and influence you can be selected to big-paying jobs.

The Secret of His Success

A young man I knew had just graduated from law school. He came to our lectures in Carnegie Hall, and asked my advice as to how he could rise rapidly in his profession. I advised him to go into local politics in his ward, to meet every politician, big or small, that he could. He began to offer his services and soon began to be known around town. In a very short time he won an office very high in the District Attorney's office, and a few short years later became one of our big city judges. He was talented, but in his case it was the groundwork he had laid for his career that elevated him to such heights so rapidly.

A young lady asked advice as to how she should handle her career. She was a secretary but wanted rapid advancement. I told her to start working with local civic betterment groups. She eventually came to the attention of the mayor, and she became one of his inner circle workers and confidants!

There is no limit to what heights you may soar if you have the vision to seek out the aid of important and influential people.

3. Join some veteran's group, or the American Legion, if you qualify, or any other group that is active in your community. Not only does this pave the way to social activity, but it can lead to an expansion of your business contacts and a position of prestige.

4. Get in the habit of writing letters to important people, suggesting ideas for the betterment of the community, or offering your help in some charitable work being undertaken. Occasionally write a letter praising the official, and he will definitely take note of you. I have known people who got in to see the heads of some of the biggest businesses in the country through this practice of letter-writing, and valuable contacts were made that later led to financial or social betterment.

How to Make Your Vacation Pay Dividends

5. Use your vacation time profitably. Plan your vacation so that you come in contact with people who might prove valuable to your career. Important and wealthy people go to such places as Florida, California, Hawaii, Canada, Monte Carlo, Switzerland, Paris, and the Riviera. It costs no more to go to places that are popular with wealthy and important people, and sometimes you can meet people who are very useful in the future. Cultivate sports such as fishing, golfing, and water sports.

Make it a point to join groups that go in for stamp collecting, hobbies and interests that you might enjoy, and which you can share with people who will have the same hobby.

Market Your Ideas

6. Do not be afraid to present your ideas to important business executives or wealthy people. They are constantly searching for new ideas, new talent, new markets. If you bring them an idea that changes their business for the better, you may work yourself right into an important position. I know one young man who sent the Canadian Pacific Railroad President a suggestion for increasing tourist trade on the Canadian Railroads, and the President instantly arranged an interview that led the young man to win a lucrative post with a Canadian Travel Agency.

7. In making contacts with important people, show interest in them and their work. Have respect for their advice and opinions. They have risen in their profession because of specialized skills; respect their judgment.

Building the Other Fellow's Ego

8. Build the other person's ego, for if he *is* important, he will appreciate recognition of that fact. Even great people have their low moments. A case in point: Mischa Elman, considered by many to be our greatest violin virtuoso, who has appeared in Carnegie Hall many times, and always sells out every performance, was sitting in a restaurant in a large city in America one day, having lunch with a friend of his. He was in a disheartened mood, for his concert had not sold as well as he'd expected it to. A waitress stopped at the table and recognized the great violinist and said, "Mr. Elman, it's such an honor to be serving you. I have some of your recordings, and I love your playing." The great violinist instantly responded with a beaming countenance, and asked the young lady's name. His entire mood changed from that moment on, and later the waitress received a package from Mischa Elman, giving her many of his recordings that she did not have.

9. When you meet people who are important and who might prove helpful, find a common ground of interest which you can use as a basis upon which to build a friendship. This might be work you have in common, school chums you both know, a sport that you can share, coin collecting, music, art, the theater, books ... any of these interests instantly establish a bond of mutuality which encourages confidence and friendship.

Which Conversational Group do You Fit?

10. Try to discuss things that are pleasant and non-controversial. Avoid politics and religion. You are judged by the things you talk about. There are three classifications of people:

(a) Those who talk mostly about people and the things they have done or are doing. This is the more common type.

(b) People who talk about things; their cars, jobs, homes, work, money. Many people operate on this level of conversation.

(c) People who talk about ideas; world conditions, ways for bettering the world; art, music, literature; the international situation, and general business matters. These people operate on a higher intellectual plane than those who talk about people or things. Find out what plane your prospective friend is, and then talk on *his level of inspiration*. Do not talk down to him, if he is on the first two planes of interest, but share those topics with him.

11. Learn how to tell good, amusing stories, without being smutty. Remember, people may laugh at off-color jokes, but when they think of you *they associate you with the obscene stories you told,* and this is *not* a pleasant association. More important than telling a good story, learn how to be a good listener.

Package Your Personality

12. Package your personality so it shows your best side. This means you should have a pleasant, affable, and relaxed personality, that is easy to get along with. Practice smiling, and learn how to have a good, hearty laugh, for a good laugh is infectious, and often helps win friends. Everyone wants to laugh; no one really wants to share your sad experiences and cry.

13. Give freely of yourself, if you wish to truly attract and hold the interest of important people. If you have nothing else of value to give the world, *give yourself,* your interest, your enthusiasm, your charm, your attention, your consideration and *most important of all,* your sincere friendship!

Take this Test to Determine If You can Win Friends and Hold Them

1. Do you enjoy meeting people?
2. Are you at ease in the presence of others?
3. Do you know how to keep a conversation going?
4. Do you show an interest in other people?
5. Do you talk about your friend's interests rather than exclusively about your own?
6. Do friends seek you out and confide in you?
7. Do you avoid criticizing or arguing with friends?
8. Do you judge your friends by the way they dress?
9. Do you remember your friends' birth dates and other important events in their lives, like anniversaries?
10. Do you help friends when they ask favors of you?

The answers to all of the above questions should be Yes. If you answered six or more questions yes, then you have great ability to win and hold friendship.

If you answer less than six yes, then you should work on your personality and increase your popularity with others.

18

Take these Seven Steps up
the Ladder of Success

There is a formula for success that is as definite as the laws that govern mathematics. When you add two and two, the sum total is four. It could never possibly be five. No matter how much you tried to distort or twist the law of mathematics, the sum still remains four.

Success is made up of several different component parts, and these are as absolute as the law of gravity. Water cannot run uphill, for it is the law of gravity for it to run down hill. Oil and water will not mix, for they are of different consistencies, different molecular structures.

So too with the laws governing success; certain elements will not mix, certain others will blend, producing the right combination for achieving success. The laws governing these elements are as fixed as the planets in the heavens. In all the lives of the great men of history, these seven elements have been present.

Mind—the Guiding Light

Your mind is the guiding light that shows you the way to the top of your ladder of success. In the Epilogue to Beaumont and Fletcher's *Honest Man's Fortune,* it is said so clearly;

> Man is his own star; and the soul that can
> Render an honest and a perfect man,
> Commands all light, all influence, all fate;

Nothing to him falls early or too late.
Our acts our angels are, or good or ill,
Our fatal shadows that walk by us still.

Your mind must cut the pattern that fits the destiny you choose. When this has once been decided on, everything else will fall into its right place. The problems and challenges of life will still be there, but you will find a way to ride over them rough-shod, and they will only serve to sharpen your wits, and increase your determination to succeed.

Step No. 1. The Desire to Achieve

Elsewhere in this study we have spoken of desire, but in connection with achieving success, it is vitally important that you use this Emotion of Desire correctly.

Everyone wants to succeed. Everyone wants fame and fortune. What you must do is *define the exact type of success you desire*.

Everyone wants to achieve the building of a million dollar fortune, but most people do not realize that this is *not enough*. The desire to have a million dollars must be fortified by the exact knowledge of *how* you wish to achieve it, and what you want the million dollars for.

This concrete image must exist in your mind first. It is the pattern by which Universal Intelligence can cut the cloth to make the suit you have chosen.

To help you crystallize your desires let us examine them in cold print.

What type of success do you desire?
What are you willing to give to life for your fulfilment of this desire?
What steps are you taking NOW to reach your goal?
Are you fully using the gifts and talents you possess?
Do you desire money so you can live a more indolent life?
Do you wish fame and fortune so you can help others?
Are your desires for progress, knowledge, happiness, good, beauty? These help crystallize your creative ability into more productive channels.

Your Mental Attitude towards Success

Your mental attitude determines the type of success you achieve. It determines whether you shall fail or not. You may have all the elements of success around you right now, in your own environment, and yet, because your mental attitude is one of failure, defeat and indolence, you may be overlooking the biggest opportunity of your entire life.

> Two men looked out from prison bars,
> One saw mud, the other stars.

Which are you seeing in life, the mud or the stars? There are both mental attitudes in existence; you may choose whichever one you wish. You can make of your life a shambles or a success. You can utilize the talents God has given you for doing something magnificent or you may create a mental hovel in which you live in ignorance, fear and hate. The choice is up to you. The desires you enthrone in your consciousness can cause you to have either a broad, comprehensive view of your future life, or a mean, petty and limited one of poverty, lack and limitation.

Millions in His Own Backyard

A farmer in Pennsylvania observed that his cattle could not drink water that came up from the springs in his backyard because of an oily, slimy scum that formed on the water. Finally, in discouragement, he sold the farm for a reasonable price and moved away. The new owner observed the same scum, and his curiosity got the best of him. He sniffed the substance and it smelled like oil. Through his curiosity that man discovered an oil field in his backyard that made him millions!

Perhaps, like this man, in the backyard of your own mind today there is an idea that can make you millions. Your mental attitude towards life and success and money, your own desires, may help unlock this secret within your mind.

Harness your desires, make them work for you. If you want the better things of life, this is fine; but do not expect life to give them to you free. You must make some effort to achieve the success you desire, and you will have taken the first step up that ladder of success.

Step No. 2. Your Dream or Inner Vision

All outward forms of creation in the man-made world began with a dream or inner vision. This is a very important part of our Million Dollar Secret. Everyone has some kind of dream of the world in which he wishes to live. This dream resides in the mind, and is instilled by our early childhood thoughts and experiences. You played house, and expressed the idea of love and marriage and having your own family some day. You played doctor or nurse, and expressed the dream you had of some day being a doctor or nurse in real life.

Dreams crystallize into reality, when you apply this formula correctly.

Voltaire said, "An idea, when it comes with the force of a revelation will lead to a revolution in your life."

The overpowering *idea you hold in your mind* about the life you wish to lead is the *dream or inner vision* that will shape your entire future. You must have this dream firmly fixed and never stray from it; otherwise you weaken the resolve of the mental force within you that could make the dream become reality.

The Peasant Girl's Dream of Fortune that Came True

I visited Greece some years ago and was entertained at the home of friends. They had a maid who worked for them. She was a peasant girl in her early forties. She was a very plain girl, almost ugly, with mousey hair, drab features, and a squat body, that was most unprepossessing and unattractive. She had already worked for this one family for ten years and there seemed no possibility that she would ever be able to rise to any higher position in life.

This girl had a strange obsession or dream. To anyone who would listen she would tell them, "Some day I will marry a rich man and go to America. I will have a big, beautiful home with thick carpets, and my own maid, and a big automobile." People used to smile in a kindly and sympathetic manner when she told them her dream, but they all thought the poor creature was obviously deluded and unsound.

When I went out to the kitchen to thank her for the beautiful meal she had prepared, she smiled and, in her broken English, told me of her impossible dream. But I didn't smile and think her deluded. I patted her on the shoulder and replied, "Yes, one day you will meet that man from America, he will fall in love with you and you will have your beautiful home and automobile."

I knew of the miracles of life, and it did not sound fantastic to me at all, this peasant girl's impossible dream.

Two years later, I was in California, and I received a wedding invitation from this girl, who had gotten my address from her former employer. She was marrying the man she had dreamed of! A few months later, in driving to San Francisco, I passed through the town where she lived. I stopped by to see her. She had married an older Greek-American, who owned a big ranch in upper California. He had a beautiful home with thick carpets and a new Cadillac car, and was rich!

What Magic Did She Use?

What magic did this Greek girl use? She used the secret power that God has given every one of His creatures; the ability to draw from the Universal Storehouse of Riches everything that we need to fulfill our destiny. She had sent out her call to Universal Intelligence, she had held her dream in her mind so long, that it crystallized all the elements of her body and soul into one great magnetic force that impelled the first person who came into her orbit, who could make her dream come true, to desire her as much as she desired him. This older man needed a good housekeeper, a companion; he had no children, he was a widower, he was lonely. In his mind was a dream and a desire for a mate who would meet his needs, and the fact she was plain, even homely meant nothing to him; at least he could be sure that no other man would try to take her away from him! Perhaps, who knows, even this fact was the inducement that was the final, determining factor in making him choose a plain woman instead of a beautiful one. This woman now has two lovely children of her own!

Are You Afraid to Dream?

Are you afraid to dream the big, beautiful, bold dream? Most people are. They daydream occasionally, but only in fits and snatches. They occasionally think, "Oh, if I were only rich," or, "If I could marry someone who would care for me." Or, "My, it would be wonderful to have my own home." But they do not have the steady, persistent dream, "I know that some day my dreams will come true. I will succeed. I will marry the one I love. I will have a home of my own. I will be rich!"

This is the secret of our second step, the Dream or Inner Vision, that can direct your feet onto those upper rungs of our Ladder of Success. The Dream must be persistently indulged; every day the thought must be focused in your mind; you must live in the dream, visualize yourself doing the things you want to do; visualize yourself being the person you wish to be; see yourself counting the money you want to have; spending it to buy beautiful things you desire. Desire and Dream go together; they are part of the mathematical formula for achievement of your life goal.

Step No. 3. Release Creative Imagination

"Imagination is more important than knowledge." This statement, by one of our greatest scientists and mathematical geniuses, Albert Einstein, is a powerful and accurate one.

Imagination helps you grow wings of the soul and soar above the crags and pitfalls of this earth, just as a jet plane soars into the skies thirty thousand feet above the earth, and ignores the mountains, rivers and other obstacles that might impede its progress on the ground.

Literally, imagination means the act or power of forming mental images of what is not present. It is also the act or power of creating new ideas as by combining previous experiences.

Creative Imagination carries you a step further however, than just forming mental images; it means to cause to come into existence, to make or originate, to cause, to produce, to bring about. When you creatively imagine something you are actually causing it to come into being, for you are *forming it first in your own mind.* The method by which it comes to pass in the outer world is a mystery. Just as man knows that a kernel of corn planted in the earth is going to produce a stalk of corn with several ears on it, but he does not know nature's secret for drawing the substance from the soil to make this new creation. The *image* or *picture* of that stalk of corn, however, is *locked within the kernel of corn.* It is its *mental concept of a stalk of corn.*

Sleep in this Bed: Become a Star

Anything that can be done to stimulate this power of creative imagination, is helpful in making the inner dream come true.

A young lady once came to my home with Nicky Hilton, son of the hotel magnate. Her name was Marilyn Novak. She told me an interesting story. She lived in a studio club where many young actresses had gotten their start. The owner of the club took her to a special room on her first night there and showed her a magnificent bed, shaped like a swan, and made of hand-carved wood, covered with gold leaf. It was magnificent. The woman told Marilyn Novak, "A famous star gave me that bed. She slept in it for years. She made as high as ten thousand dollars a week. Every girl who has ever slept in it and made a wish to become a star, has had her wish come true. Tonight's your turn." When the girl finished telling me her story, she turned her big trusting eyes up to me and asked, "Do you believe in such things? I'm waiting for its magic to work for me."

I replied, "It will work for you, if you *believe it*."

A few months later I read that Columbia studios had just signed a contract with a young girl named Marilyn Novak. They changed her name to Kim Novak, and the fable of the Golden Swan came true, for she did become one of Hollywood's brightest stars.

Imagination Controls the World

It is in imagination that man has one of the greatest forces in the universe. It is through his imagination that man controls the world. See the enormous network of airlines that girdle the globe; this concept of mass travel by air, at the speed of sound, was first a concept in some man's imagination before it became a reality.

Some primitive man first saw a rolling stone, and in his imagination he visualized it attached to a cart; thus was the wheel born. Scientists call this one of the greatest inventions of all time. From it came all our modern industrial machinery, and even the airplane itself could never have existed without this first concept of a wheel.

In his imagination, the first man who saw a bird fly, and imaged a flying machine, used the creative power of the mind through his creative imagination. The world has expanded enormously since man began to use the creative power of his imagination.

"The human race" Napoleon said, "is governed by its imagination."

Begin today to create the world in which you wish to live through the power of your creative imagination. Picture the things you want to do, hold them in consciousness, try to pattern your actions in such a way that they are constantly working towards the fulfilment of the goals you hold in your imagination.

Florenz Ziegfeld created his glorified Follies by having a tremendous imagination. Barnum founded his great circus by building an imaginative concept of greatness in the mind of the public. Disney created Disneyland by having an imagination that encompassed some of the most daring ideas in modern entertainment. People from all over the world go to see the magical fairyland he has created with the expenditure of millions of dollars *and creative imagination!*

Step No. 4. The Power of Concentration

A lightning bolt can split a giant oak tree because of its concentrated power.

A ruby cannot be melted in the hottest of furnaces, but if it is placed in a glass cube that concentrates the sun's rays on it for a few hours, it can be turned into liquid!

The power of concentration is terrific when it is released in your mind. Most people scatter their mental energy and force by spending ninety per cent of their time in thinking over past defeats and disappointments. Their minds spend hours in dwelling on the negative aspects of their lives, the failures, the tragedies, the sickness, the accidents, the lost investments they have had in the past. This tendency to concentrate on the negative aspects of life only helps inscribe these things deeper into the convolutions of the brain.

Reverse, Do Not Rehearse Your Failures

In using the positive power of concentration learn to reverse your failures, not rehearse them by constant repetition, for in thinking of them or talking of your failures and misery you only tend to make them more real in your mind.

How many times a day do you think of your lacks and limitations? How many times do you tell people about your failures?

How often do you find yourself thinking or saying, "That was a terrible thing that happened to me! My life has never been anything but misery and failure! I cannot succeed because I don't have a college education. I can never become rich because I have no ability. I am too old to start again in life. I can never go into my own business for there are no opportunities left."

This process of negative thinking is what I call "rehearsing the negative aspects of life." This habit tends to short-circuit the power of the battery of your mind and builds the habit patterns of failure, misery and unhappiness so firmly in your consciousness that it is difficult to ever break them.

How to Concentrate

How can you concentrate your mental power upon the achievement of fame and fortune? The mind must be held steadily to the goal, and not allowed to waiver or falter.

"Successful minds work like a gimlet—to a single point," Bovee said. This is true; no one and nothing must be allowed to interfere with your mental concentration. Pick definite times each day and sit quietly by yourself concentrating your mental power on what it is you're trying to achieve. Practice this art of concentration until it becomes a habit.

The Chinese have an exercise to acquire the gift of concentration. They pass by a store window and with one glance try to see how many objects they can fix in their minds and recall later. They keep this up until they are able to recall as many as one hundred objects they have observed in a single glance!

Practice holding your mind steady and still on one thought. Allow no other thought to enter your mind. Do this for several seconds at a time, until you are able to concentrate on one thought for at least five minutes or more.

Then every day give yourself a mental exercise in concentration. Sit quietly and concentrate on the things you want to accomplish for that day; the people you want to see; the money you wish to attract; the sales you want to make. As you hold each separate thought in your mind, give it all the concentrated power you can summon up from your mind, before going on to another thought or idea.

Step No. 5. Using the Power of Intuition

The humming bird needs no instructor in the art of construct-ing his thistle-down-lined, swinging nest. Something within him *knows how to construct it perfectly!* The ant requires no one to tell him how to organize his nest and build an anthill. This is an intuitive function with its mind.

This step up the Ladder of Success is a vitally important one. You may be striving so hard to achieve fulfilment of your life-goal that you have lost sight of the fact a higher mind within you knows more about this matter than you can ever learn.

"We know what we are, but know not what we may be," Shake-speare wrote. It is true, we know our limitations, our failures, our blundering ways of doing things, but seldom do we stop to think of *what we may be*. The superconscious mind within you knows how to guide you to the fulfilment of your destiny. Every genius of history has been able to tap this hidden power of the intuitive mind within and use it to achieve greatness.

Listen to the Voice within

A ten-year-old boy came up to Schubert after one of his concerts and told him of his desire to become a great composer. He asked Schubert how he could achieve his goal. The master told him to begin with simple themes first and gradually go on to more diffi-cult compositions.

The boy told him however, that he wanted to compose full-scale concertos and symphonies. He said to Schubert, "When you were ten you were able to compose great things."

The talented composer replied, "Yes, but I did not ask HOW."

You have within your mind an intelligence that **knows** more than you will ever learn. Listen to the voice within; it is intuition trying to guide you to fulfilment of your dream.

Emerson spoke of this Intuitive Mind Within in these brilliant words:

A man should learn to detect and watch that gleam of light which flashes across his mind from within, more than the lustre of the firmament of bards and sages. Yet, he dismisses without notice his thought, because it is his. In every work of genius we recognize our own rejected thoughts; they come back to us with a certain alienated majesty. Trust thyself; every heart vibrates to that iron string.

Consult this inner mind whenever you are in doubt. Go into solitude and there ask this higher mind what you should do in any given situation. Then wait for the answer to come through. The thought that most persistently rises in your mind is generally the correct one. It's amazing how seldom is this intuitive mind wrong. If you look back on your life, see how many times this higher mind told you not to do something; if you went against its advice, you lived to regret it! It knows, for the omniscience of God is in every atom and cell of the entire creation. It resides in your brain, because you are a part of the creative intelligence that animates the entire universe.

Step No. 6. Build Habit Patterns of Success

It is just as easy to build habit patterns of success as of failure. All great men built such habit patterns in their minds. They could never have achieved success if they had not applied this vital principle to their lives.

Ask yourself these questions:

> Are you efficient?
> Are you punctual?
> Are you honest?
> Do you give full value?
> Are you positive?
> Are you confident?
> Are you thrifty?
> Do you know how to handle money?
> Are you able to organize people?
> Are you outgoing in your personality?
> Are you orderly, clean, neat?
> Do you recognize big ideas?
> Do you persist in the face of obstacles?
> Do you believe in yourself?
> Do you think and talk **only** success?

Study the above questions carefully, for each is a key to the building of new habit patterns of success. No life that violates these principles and rules of success can ever be said to be outstanding or successful.

"Habits start as cobwebs," someone has said, "and end as chains." Nothing is so deadly as a negative thought or act persistently indulged. Victims of cigarette smoking, dope addiction or alcoholism know too well the truth of this statement. Finally the habit becomes so firmly entrenched in the mind that it is almost impossible to eradicate.

Build Your Future on Positive Habits

Make it a point to indulge *only positive thoughts,* and you will gradually, step by step, build your entire future on positive habits. You must substitute a positive thought for every negative thought you hold in your mind at present. Examine these thoughts you have built in consciousness, and then, if they reflect fear, worry, hate, failure, old-age, sickness, poverty, or limitation, carefully choose an *opposite thought of a positive nature* and substitute it in its place.

Soon you will find it's impossible to think in terms of failure, inadequacy and incompetence. Daily begin the practice of acting as though you are already a success; wear your best clothes, have your shoes brightly polished, keep your hands and nails clean, wear your brightest smile, go forth each day expectantly, as though you are sure you will meet with golden opportunities all during that day, and you will be building positive mental and physical habits which will soon become as much a part of you as your arms and legs.

Step No. 7. Have Faith in Your Destiny

Faith in yourself and faith in your destiny—this is an essential and important step in your climb up the ladder of success. Many talented people never make it because they do not have this essential ingredient of our Million Dollar Secret.

An author named Howard Fast wrote a book some years ago. He sent it out to several publishers. They all turned it down. No one had faith in it. Fast had such faith in the ultimate success of his book that he raised one thousand dollars and published it himself. Only a few hundred copies existed, and undoubtedly, at that time, for a very small sum, anyone could have bought the movie rights to his book.

Then one day a producer read the book, and offered Fast a large sum for the movie rights. *Spartacus* was the name of the book that Howard Fast had faith in. It became one of the great motion pictures of our time.

You May Walk with Princes and Kings

In the realm of mind you are as great as any man who ever lived. You may walk with princes and kings in the realm of intellect and thought. Your ideas are as precious as those that were brought forth from some of the greatest minds of the ages. A Plato or Socrates, a Voltaire or Shakespeare, a Newton or a Jefferson may slumber within the innermost recesses of your own mind. Have faith in this power that lies within you.

When Leonardo da Vinci was young he was haunted by the idea that he was illegitimate. Everyone told him that this stigma would always keep him from achieving greatness. He set about when he was very young to find a way to overcome this limitation of birth. He chose painting as a talent which he might develop into such creative genius that he might one day walk with princes and kings. With this incentive, and the faith this thought inspired within his mind, Leonardo da Vinci went on to produce such masterpieces as the Mona Lisa, and the Last Supper, and, indeed, he did walk with princes and kings, for he associated with the crowned heads of Europe during his lifetime. They all recognized his great genius.

Faith in Yourself the Open Sesame

Faith in yourself is the "open sesame" to riches and fame. It matters not that others lack faith in you or your works; if you really believe in yourself and your talents, you will build inspiration and power to persist until you have achieved your life goal.

"All things are possible to him that believeth."

The Bible states this great truth very simply but forcibly. You can achieve anything you really, sincerely desire, and that you dream of attaining, if you have faith in yourself, and faith in your Divine Destiny, which is different from every other person who ever lived.

Points to Remember

1. Keep your eye on the ultimate goal at the top of your Ladder of Success, not on the obstacles you must pass to reach the top.

2. Do not confide your secret innermost dreams to unsympathetic people. They may laugh at you and discourage you.

3. Overcome discouragement and disappointment by realizing that every day begins a fresh, blank page in your Book of Destiny. Inscribe upon it what you wish.

4. Day-dream, but also be sure to act; for dreams without action never achieve fulfilment.

5. Pick worthwhile goals in life; not the cheap, tawdry, sensational or debasing things that are not worthy of you.

6. Imitate the greatness of others, until you stamp upon all your creative efforts your own stamp of originality.

7. Start an action towards your goal first in your mind; then the Law of Action and Reaction will cause you to gravitate in the direction of that goal.

19

Accept Abundance—
the Philosophy of Riches

Someone has said, "Most people are always getting ready to live, but they never really live."

Is this true about you? Are you always planning on what you will do when you have that first million dollars? Do you keep putting off that vacation you want to take, the trip to visit your family, the trip to Europe? Are you constantly reminding yourself of the wonderful things you are going to do when you retire?

If so, then you are not applying the philosophy of our Million Dollar Secret to your life. It is in the eternal *now* that you must live. It is *now* that you must accept abundance. *Now* is the right time to make that move to another house, to a better job, to a bigger income.

"But how?" you may ask, for all about you are the evidences of your inability to make such radical changes. If this is true in your life, then I want you to study this chapter over and over, until the philosophy of the Million Dollar Secret is so deeply ingrained in your mind that you will never forget it.

As Rich as You Think You are

I once knew a man who had made a million dollars in California real estate. He had moved into the Wilshire Boulevard district in the depression years and bought up many lots. He saw real estate boom and sold at the highest prices. When I met him he was already in his early sixties. I said to him, "Now, with all your money, you can take it easy and begin to do some of the things you've always wanted to do with money."

Do you know this man's answer? He said, "Oh, no, I can't stop now. I feel very insecure with only a million. I need at least two million more to back it up."

Two years later this man died of a heart attack! He never lived to enjoy his money.

A famous movie star, Clark Gable, had a strenuous life. He accumulated a fortune, and when he was in his middle-age, he could have taken a well-earned rest and enjoyed his sports and hobbies. Do you know what he told me one day at lunch? "I have a baby coming. I've got to keep making pictures to secure his future. I don't have enough to retire."

A year later Clark Gable was dead; he never lived to see the little son who was on the way. He left over a million dollars!

With this type of philosophy regarding riches, *no man is ever satisfied* with what he has! This is the secret I want to share with you. *You will never have enough money to satisfy you!*

You are as rich as you think you are! You can begin this moment, no matter what financial circumstances you are in, to think, act, look and live like a *millionaire!*

Accept the Abundance about You

Right here and now, if you will look about you, in whatever circumstances you are in, you are richer than many people. You can begin to accept the abundance that is all about you in this moment and *feel that you are rich*. If you have your health, this is worth more than a million dollars. The late John D. Rockefeller, with all his hundreds of millions, had an artificial stomach and couldn't enjoy a good steak! You can enjoy your food, you can sleep well at night, your conscience is clear, you do not have to worry about being imprisoned for taxes you owe the government, you can enjoy your wife and children, your friends and neighbors, without being excessively rich.

I remember one day I was at a barber shop having a haircut. I saw a pompous, obviously rich and important man next to me, and the whole shop was dancing attendance on him. He had the works; from manicure to shoeshine, massage, shampoo, everything. He wore a huge diamond tiepin in the shape of a horseshoe; his clothes were expensively tailored. When he left he gave everyone a dollar tip.

The shoeshine boy said enviously, "Boy, I wish I could change places with that guy!"

The barber who had waited on him said, "You do? Do you know who that guy is? He's a big-shot gambler and racketeer. His young wife recently ran off with another man. His six year old boy was killed by a drunken driver, he has ulcers and a very bad heart condition. His money can buy him everything but health, love, happiness, peace of mind, and heaven!"

Live in the Eternal Now

There is the answer to man's eternal, unending quest for more and more material treasures. There is the philosophy of riches; never want more than you can conveniently use; never wait for a more opportune moment to begin to live the life you desire; do not put off living until some future day when you have more money, more time, better circumstances. *That time may never come!* Live in the eternal now. This is the future of which you dreamed all through your yesterdays. There is *no other future but this moment,* as far as you know, so live it up fully, and enjoy every second of it, spend the money you have, and depend on the knowledge in this book to keep a steady stream of riches flowing through your life, blessing you, enriching you, and then going on to enrich the world.

Money Is Like a Flowing River

Andrew Carnegie said of fortune; "It will some day be considered a sin for men to die rich." He made hundreds of millions of dollars, but he had the fun of spending most of them while he was alive. He gave it away; to charities, twelve hundred public libraries, museums, art galleries, educational institutions. He enjoyed making money, he lived fully and well every moment, and he had the additional fun of sharing his riches. That is the philosophy of our Million Dollar Secret.

There is nothing wrong with making money, having a fortune and spending it. The Bible does not say money is evil, it says "The *love* of money is the root of all evil." In the second chapter of Genesis, twenty-eighth verse it also says, "And God looked upon the gold of the land and saw that it was good." What is good, cannot be evil, but it can be *used for destructive purposes*. And gold, when it is selfishly used or monopolized is a canker of the soul that can destroy individuals or nations. Money is like a flowing river, it must flow in and through your life, and then go on to bless others.

The Fate of the Ten Richest Men in the World

During the depression years there were ten of the richest men in the world, whose lives had been made up by a quest for gold. They never knew when to stop. They achieved their billions of dollars, and they ruled industry, chemicals, financial institutions. Do you want to know what happened to them? Each of these men who literally worshiped gold, and had little time to enjoy life, wound up suicides, imprisoned for fraud, broke, or in other ways disgraced. *Not one knew when to stop and begin to live!*

Now, this sad statistic does not mitigate against the philosophy of the Million Dollar Secret: Make all the money you want, legitimately and wisely, but while you're doing this, Live! Live! Live!

What Keeps You from Attracting Abundance?

There are several forces that fight man's acquisition of wealth and supply. If you know what keeps you from attracting abundance, you can set to work at once to remove these restraining forces and accept abundance here and now.

1. **Fear of riches.** Most people are afraid to think they could ever become wealthy! They have been so used to the idea that they were born poor and must remain poor that they forget the world is teeming with abundance; all they need do is accept it! Under every square mile of the earth's surface, science says, there are literally *millions of dollars worth of treasures!* The government will give away *millions of acres of land,* for those who care to go out to a Western homestead. All they need do is to write to the government for literature on this subject. The Northwest is teeming with riches in lumber and agricultural products, if people really want to get away from the squalor of tenements and the poverty of the over-crowded cities.

But most people are afraid to take the chance of giving up a good-paying job, which they hate, and risk getting some other work, or striking out on their own in a new business, a new location, or a strange environment. Remove *fear,* and you will begin to move towards your rightful place in the economic scale of life.

2. **Greed and selfishness.** These two emotions are negative, and motivate millions of people. When we have greed and selfishness as dominating emotions they tend to cripple our minds and blind us to the true values of life.

An Oriental farmer once went to a fair. There he saw a magician turning beans into gold. His greed got the best of him, and he thought, "If I could have that secret I'd be a rich man."

He offered the magician his farm and all he owned, for the secret. The magician made him sign the deed, giving him his land, and then proceeded to show him the magic secret that would turn the beans to gold.

He held a bean in his fingers and dropped it, at the same time he said the magic word, "Abacadabra" and, presto! the bean had changed into a shining nugget of purest gold!

The farmer was delighted. He grabbed the bag of beans and started away, but the magician stopped him and said, "Oh, I forgot to tell you, one part of the magic formula. When you say the magic word 'Abacadabra,' you must *not at the same time think of a white elephant!* If you do, it will ruin the magic."

The farmer smiled and said, "Oh, that will be easy." And rushed from the tent.

Later, when he was home, he pulled down all the blinds, sat at a table, rubbing his hands together greedily, picked up a bean, said the word "Abacadabra," and as he was about to drop it, he thought, "Now, I must not think of a white elephant." But he *had thought of a white elephant* in doing this, and as the bean hit the table, he saw, with dismay, that it remained a bean!

Again and again he tried the magic formula, and each time he thought of the white elephant, until he was nearly crazy with frustration and anger.

The White Elephants of Life

A fable, but a true one. The white elephants of fear, frustration, greed, selfishness, hate, monopoly, envy, resentment, jealousy, and avarice rise before our eyes and blur our vision when we try to manifest riches and abundance. We must get rid of these white elephants that haunt our minds before we can accept abundance.

3. **Ignorance.** Here is one of life's most fatal diseases. It infects the social body of our times, and makes million of people poor. It is *not economic poverty* that makes half our nation live in substandard conditions; it is ignorance of the laws of nature. You have more abundance than you can use, but man-made laws of production and distribution doom half the people to live in eternal poverty.

Wasted Resources

Did you know that this country produces more than enough of butter, milk, eggs, oranges, potatoes, and meat to feed the entire world? And yet, the populations in India, China, Japan, Africa and many other parts of the world never know what it is to get enough to eat. What happens to the over-abundance of food we produce in this great country? I have seen thousands of gallons of milk poured into the Los Angeles River, to keep the prices high. I have seen millions of tons of oranges and potatoes burned, to keep the tables of America empty of these commodities and hold up the high prices. You pay nearly a dollar a pound for butter, but the government is paying millions of dollars a day for storage of butter. Their answer to the question "Why?" is that it is an economic necessity to produce less food, for if too much is produced, the farmer does not get a fair price for his crops, and will suffer. This is a poor argument and is due to the ignorance of nature's laws of supply and demand. There is an abundance of everything man needs to feed billions of people, but ignorance holds man back from *accepting the abundance* that God has created for all his creatures.

Wisdom is the Answer

You can acquire knowledge and wisdom to cope with the world in which you live. You cannot stop the march of time, but your little addition to the wisdom and knowledge of the world can eventually work to elevate the standards of the world and bring peace, plenty and abundance to every human being who lives.

An ancient Arabian proverb states:

Men are four;
He who knows not and knows
not he knows not, he is a
fool—shun him;
He who knows not and knows
he knows not, he is simple—
teach him;
He who knows and knows not he knows,
he is asleep—
wake him.
He who knows and knows he knows,
he is wise—follow him!

4. **Laziness.** There is a scientific word, *abulia,* which is very beautiful, but which means lazy or indolent. This very often keeps people from coming into the abundance which is all around them. Such people develop an inefficient personality, that makes them shabby and careless. No one wants them around, because they contribute nothing to progress or life. Laziness is a disease that can be cured. A good constructive program of activity that one likes, is a sure cure for laziness. A desire to accumulate money, to become famous, to achieve something outstanding, all help overcome this tendency to be idle and live in poverty.

5. **Low standards.** It's amazing how many thousands of people live in shabby, ugly surroundings, because their standards are so low and they do nothing about elevating them. This is due to early childhood training, or sheer shiftlessness. Such people can only be shaken from their mental and physical lethargy by arousing in them a sincere desire to better their surroundings and circumstances. You know the saying, "You can remove a pig from his sty, but you cannot remove the sty from the pig." Such people complain because of their limited circumstances, but actually, if the truth were known, they would not change even if placed in the most fortunate circumstances.

Peasants and Palaces

In the days of the Russian revolution the peasants were victorious over the czarist forces and moved into the palaces. They fed their horses out of the fine rosewood pianos, tore down the valuable tapestries from the walls, ripped them up and made blankets for their horses. They broke up the hand-carved antique furniture and built fires on the marble floors. They lacked the awareness of the priceless treasures they were destroying because they had never had an opportunity to develop appreciation for beauty and art.

The Riches that Exist All about You

Right this moment you are richer than any potentate of the Far East was in ancient times. With all their millions they could never have had a radio, a television set, a jet plane, a subway, automobile, or a tape recorder or record player. Think what such a rich potentate would have given to see a spectacle on the screen like Cinerama! You have the glory of motion pictures for a very small sum, and on TV, they are free.

You possess the greatness of magnificent opera houses like the Metropolitan Opera in New York, you may see and hear musical geniuses like Leopold Stokowski, Leonard Bernstein, and, on records, such great conductors as Toscanini, and Bruno Walter. You can still hear the glorious voices of Caruso, Flagstad, Schumann-Heink, and Chaliapin, even though they are gone. You may pick up your telephone and call Europe or the West Coast in a few seconds time and clearly hear the voices of your friends and loved ones.

There are riches all about you, if you have the vision to see them and be aware of them. These riches are *yours* here and now. You do not need millions to own these priceless treasures. All you need do is *accept abundance!*

The Priceless Treasures of the Ages

You may have the priceless treasures of the ages for the asking. In New York, the Metropolitan Museum of Art has some of the world's greatest art treasures. In every big city there are fine museums, galleries, free public exhibitions on loan from other museums. All these things are yours to enjoy and view, without charge.

Then think of the priceless treasures of all ages that exist in your free public libraries. There you may browse in the comfort and luxury of the company of the greatest intellects of all time. The philosophy, history, art, music, poetry, drama, and literature of the ages is stored for your inquiring mind. Enrich yourself with these *free gifts of life.* You do not need a fortune to enjoy these luxuries.

Do You Desire an Estate?

Perhaps you desire an estate? Have you stopped to visit your own city parks recently? In New York City, we have Central Park, hundreds of acres, beautifully preserved for the people. I often walk there and visualize it as being my own personal estate. The only difference is that I do not have to hire hundreds of gardeners to look after it. This is all done for me. I also have a private zoo in the park which I enjoy immensely. Think what a bother it would be if you owned a zoo and had to feed the animals and clean all the cages! Yet, these *free* parks and *free* zoos, and botanical gardens that most cities support, are literally yours. With millions of dollars you could never afford such vast estates and zoos.

"But," you may say, "these things are *not mine!*" To that I reply, "Is anything really yours?" Henry Ford died and left a fortune of five hundred million dollars. Was it actually his? *He had to leave it behind!*

Enjoy All the Good Things of Life

Use and enjoy all the great free gifts of life, and as you acquire the habit of accepting abundance, you will find that your own powers of appreciation and acquisitiveness will grow until you are able to attract your own fortune, and have your own estates, libraries, art treasures and luxuries that you purchase.

A famous philosopher said of life and its treasures:

Remember that you ought to behave in life as you would at a banquet. As something is being passed around it comes to you; stretch out your hand, take a portion of it politely. It passes on; do not detain it. Or, it has not come to you yet; do not project your desire to meet it, but wait until it comes in front of you. So act toward children, so toward a wife, so toward office, so toward wealth.

Enjoy all the good things of life, take them as they come; do not strive too desperately for the millions you want. Use the laws and principles given in this book, for they will work to bring you riches, peace of mind, health, happiness, and enjoyment, but if nature doesn't dump a million dollar fortune into your lap, do not think she has failed you, nor that this book and its philosophy has failed; there are values in this world that are worth more than a million dollars, and you may have these priceless treasures here and now without having to wait for them. Take the free gifts of friendship, love, happiness, beautiful music, gorgeous sunsets, nature's beauty, bird song, oceans, rivers and lakes, mountains and deserts, music and poetry. These magnificent treasures are spread before you on the festive board of life. Partake freely! They are yours for the asking. Accept Abundance! It is all about you, if you but have eyes to see and ears to hear the universal song of abundance.

20

Think on these Great Things

If I ask you to visualize yourself having a million dollars, it is difficult for you to conceive such a figure. If I say one thousand dollars, it is easier for the average person to conceive of it, for he has undoubtedly had that much money or more at some time in his life.

If I tell you to expand your thinking to include a billion stars in the heavens and the trillions of light years it takes the light from these stars to reach the earth, it is apt to stagger your imagination and tire it. Big things often obstruct the working of the mind and cause it to resist the achievement of fame, fortune or greatness.

Expand Your Thinking to Greatness

The Bible says, "Think on these things." Let us add the word "great" and expand our thinking to Greatness. Most people are so used to thinking of small sums of money, little success, limited opportunities, petty efforts, that they often restrict their own growth and limit their achievements in life.

In order to take your mind from the finite and limited, to the infinite and unlimited, I am going to select some of man's greatest and most outstanding achievements in history, and ask you to expand your thinking to these great accomplishments. Study these great things, imitate the inspiration that caused them to be created, emulate the process of reasoning and logic that went into their creation. You can bask in the reflected glory of the creative imaginations of the great ones of history, and eventually, as you contemplate these vast works, discoveries, inventions and industrial achievements, your own mind will begin to imitate the processes used by these great geniuses, and you will start to create your own great works.

Greatness through Association

Your mind grows stronger and greater through association of ideas. Your concepts expand enormously by dwelling on the great creative achievements of all ages. Just as a magnet grows stronger when it is given a steel bar to hold, so too your mind grows stronger when you pass through its structure the magnificent achievements of the great men of history and the tremendous works they have created. You can borrow greatness from the great. You can imitate the processes they have used to create great works of art, literature, invention, drama, science, medicine, law, and industry. Their secrets may be your secrets, for when you think big things, you will have the faith to achieve big things! Someone has said, "It is impossible to imitate Voltaire without being Voltaire."

Greatest Achievement of Ancient Times

The pyramids of Egypt were built nearly four thousand years before the time of Christ. Standing in the midst of the Egyptian desert is the Pyramid of Cheops, built by the ancient Pharaohs as a memorial and tomb for the rulers of Egypt. Enormous stone blocks tower about two hundred feet high. These stones were carved from a quarry and hauled to the building sites by slaves. There was no machinery, such as we have today to lift these enormous granite blocks into place.

Try to visualize the system used by the ancient Egyptians to raise those mammoth stones into place. Some believe that runways were built, which gradually rose higher and higher, and that the blocks of stone were pulled up the steep inclines with ropes.

Let this Great Project Stir Your Imagination

Search for the key to the building of the pyramids and then apply that secret to the creation of your own great works. Let this great project stir your imagination. Ponder on the greatness of the pyramids and then let it be an incentive for building a fortune, for attaining fame, honors and glory in your own life. Sit and visualize the means that you will use to draw attention to your work, to bring out your own great talent. Let the patience and perseverance that was used to create that monumental work be the mainspring of action in your life that causes you to strive to achieve your dream.

The Acropolis of Greece

One of the most magnificent creations of the human mind was the building of the Acropolis of Ancient Greece. On this imposing site is the Parthenon, known as one of the architectural triumphs of all time. The architect Pericles is credited with having conceived and built this giant, many-columned structure. It took sixteen years to build, and was created as a Temple to the ancient Gods.

In running this amazing project through your own mind and in expanding your consciousness, try to see the function and purpose of this original temple. Elevated on a promontory, high above the city of Athens, the Parthenon may be seen from all sea and land approaches to Athens. It is a symbol of the majesty and might of ancient Greece. It represents the flowering of civilization, of culture, and of the philosophy of Plato, Aristotle and Socrates.

The Realm of Inspiration

Let the Acropolis inspire your mind with the grandeur and nobility of that golden age of glory and beauty. Let it serve as an inspiration in building your future destiny as a magnificent Temple, dedicated to the principles of justice, goodness, beauty, peace, truth and love. No mind that has ever contemplated this majestic temple can ever again live in the awareness of defeat, degradation, despair or that which is debased. It lifts the spirits into a realm of inspiration that is close to the divine. It gives you a pattern to follow in building your own life, which encompasses all that is dignified, lofty and noble in the human consciousness.

The Great Wall of China

Centuries ago, in ancient China, one of the Emperors decided that he would build a great wall that would protect China from the invading hordes of Mongolia. This ruler began building this wall and succeeding rulers carried the work on for six hundred

years, using the labor of three million men to construct a wall as
long as from New York City to Kansas City, which was sixteen
hundred miles long, several feet wide and over fifteen feet high.

There is enough building material in the great Wall of China
to build a home of four or five rooms for *every family in the world!*
Stop and think of this when you begin to feel there isn't enough
abundance in the world for you to have your own home.

Duplicate the Determination and Courage this Wall Took

Duplicate the determination and courage this wall took to build.
Let your mind dwell on this incredible feat. Take into consideration the purpose and determination back of this project. Let it
inspire you, and point out how in your own life there must be
planning, direction and purpose in back of everything you do.

Of course this enormous project failed in its purpose for the
invading armies easily climbed over it. However, even this defeat
can teach you a lesson—to have direction with purpose, back of
your life, and to conserve your time, energies, money and life-
force, spending these things carefully, and applying them constructively to creating something magnificent in your own life.

Digging the Panama Canal

Certainly one of the great man-made wonders of this age was
the building of the Panama Canal, to connect the east and west
coasts of America, so ships would not have to take the long voyage
necessary to get from one ocean to another.

Visualize an enormous artificial waterway, Gatun Lake, fifty
feet above sea level, created so that locks could be flooded to lift
ships from one side of the canal to the other, where they could
then proceed on to the ocean. Giant mountains straddled this area
and they had to be cut down first. Millions of tons of earth had
to be removed, thousands of men risked death and disaster; many
were stricken with malaria, but still the great work continued. The
daring, courage and vision of men triumphed over the elemental
forces of earth, and created one of the great wonders of our age.

Apply this Inspiration to Your Life

Expand your consciousness to encompass this phenomenon, then apply the inspiration to your own life and career. What one generation of men has accomplished, you may also achieve. The spirit and vision that made the Panama Canal possible, are still in existence in the hearts and minds of men today. Become infused with this dream of greatness and realize that obstacles may straddle your pathway to achievement, but your ingenuity and persistence will serve to cut through them or circumnavigate these obstructions and attain your ultimate goal.

No one has ever attained his dream easily. Always there has been blood, sweat and tears to mark the pathway to great achievement. The higher the goal you set for yourself, the more you can be sure life will place obstacles in your path. It takes God only two months to make a pumpkin, but a hundred years to create a giant oak! Is yours a pumpkin-destiny or an oak-destiny? Persevere, and know that your rewards will be commensurate with your effort.

Man's Majestic Flight into Space

When man became weary with crawling in his oxcarts and covered wagons, slow buses and trains, over mountains and valleys and streams, he suddenly grew wings and soared into the heavens on a golden journey into the space age. Step by step he had climbed the lofty mountains that lifted him high above the dark valleys of superstition, fear and ignorance. Now his vision was unlimited, and encompassed worlds beyond this little planet earth. For the first time in history, man aimed at the very stars in the diadem of night!

With the dream came the means for fulfilment. One bright day, at the turn of the century, two men stood beside a winged giant on a little hill in the south. They dared to believe that the first heavier-than-air machine would fly. What a tremendous step forward this was! How the Wright brothers' hearts must have raced with anticipation, enthusiasm, and just a little fear, as they climbed into the open cockpit and throttled the motor. Then they felt the pulsating throb of their flimsy plane, as it roared down the field; with a sudden lurch it rose off the ground, and hurtled towards the sun! This giant bird remained aloft and passed over winged creatures, who looked in astonishment at this man-made eagle.

Then, after its brief flight, the ship landed safely and man had launched himself into the age of miracles—the unbelievable jet and space age!

Man's Most Audacious Achievement

This, one of man's most daring and audacious achievements, changed the entire course of destiny for us all. Let this great step forward serve as a stimulus to your own imagination. As you struggle in the shadow-filled valleys of routine work, hardship, poverty and limitation, do not accept the defeats and discouragements of your life. You may feel imprisoned by a job you do not like, by circumstances that hinder you, and you may long to escape into the stratosphere of freedom and opportunity that beckons you. As you look at the towering mountains of superstition, fear and ignorance that rise before you, be inspired to grow wings of the imagination and soar above the physical and material obstructions that impede your progress.

You need not remain in these dark valleys of discontent and defeat. You can mount on wings of the soul and rise above any known limitations of life. Men have achieved greatness even though crippled, blind, deaf or otherwise physically handicapped. If you expand your consciousness and have a big dream or vision, you will find the means to achieve it.

The Splitting of the Atom

An invisible realm of vast power exists all about you. Science now says that if the potential power that is locked up in an ordinary lead pencil could be released, it could level a city the size of New York!

With the splitting of the atom, science made vast steps forward in releasing and using power. This released power will eventually run our industrial machinery, our automobiles and planes, and release man from the bondage of arduous labor. It will be harnessed to convert salt water into fresh water. Our desert places will then bloom like gardens, producing more than sufficient to feed the entire world of several billion people of the distant future.

Strive to expand your own concept of life and power. Become aware of the vast, invisible realms that exist beyond man's physical vision and which are only revealed by the modern electronic microscope. Realize that your own mind is a storehouse of enormous powers that you still have not tapped. Try to visualize the many extensions and uses of your own mental power to the various fields of activity about you. Envision the release of your frozen assets, the big ideas that are in your mind, which can be converted into material wealth and creativity. The most powerful forces in the world, like the atom, electricity, magnetism, and capillary attraction are invisible. Tap all these forces within your own mind; let your brain be like a divine cyclotron, splitting the atoms of mind into their component parts and releasing their inspiration, beauty and creative power in glorious deeds of conquest.

Your Hidden Sources of Power

Man's dream of reaching the moon and other planets is now a reality because of the release of this hidden power of the invisible atom. Now let this daring achievement by man serve as an inspiration to you, to release your hidden sources of power, and harness them for your own constructive good.

What are some of these sources of hidden power?

Your dreams, which will motivate you in the direction of the things you dream about.

Your positive emotions, such as faith, desire, love, and generosity, are the hidden mainsprings of your nature, and when their constructive power is released in your daily activities, you will see miracles occurring in your own life. There is atomic radiation in the power of love; it is one of the most constructive emotions in the world. Its opposite, hate, is destructive. Learn how to harness your emotional drives and direct them towards high achievement and goal fulfilment. You will then have turned on a dynamo of hidden power which can carry you to the highest pinnacles of success.

Transmute Base Metal to Gold

The ancient alchemist's dream of transmuting base metal to gold has at last been achieved by scientists. By rearranging the atoms and molecules of certain metals, scientists have at last been able to create gold in small quantities.

This secret power may be used to help you convert the base

metal of failure, unhappiness, misery, discontent and poverty into the shimmering gold of achievement, happiness, contentment and abundance. Re-arrange the priceless secret chemicals and atoms of thought into new patterns, harness the imagination and let it serve as a catalyst in changing the elements of your life into bright, new products of usefulness, riches, comfort and joy. A catalyst in chemistry, as you know, is an agent that can help in the speeding up of a chemical reaction by adding a substance which itself is not changed thereby. Your imagination is such a powerful aid in the speeding up or changing of the circumstances of your life. Science is beginning to find out, in the study of the effect of the emotions and mind on health, that many people are made sick by the power of their imaginations. And many people are using this psychological principle to restore health to their bodies.

New Legs for Old

This power of transmutation through the hidden action of mind was powerfully shown in two illustrations from medical science. Glenn Cunningham, at the age of twelve received painful and crippling burns that destroyed his leg muscles almost completely. The doctors said he would never walk again, even if it were possible to save his legs. The young boy was determined he would walk and run, and every day he imagined himself playing, walking, running as other children did. He kept saying over and over to himself, "I will walk. I will run."

Then the doctors observed a strange miracle taking place before their very eyes. Under the will and determination and *imagery* of this boy's mind, the muscles of his legs became completely restored. Soon he was up and around, and a few years later, at Madison Square Garden, Glenn Cunningham ran the fastest mile in the history of sports!

Rebuild Your Body with this Power

This hidden power of mind can completely rebuild the human body. Early in this century a young woman by the name of Annette Kellerman was saddened by the fact that she had been born with a body that was misshapen and unattractive. She set to work with the only power at her disposal to change her body into a shapely, perfect one. This was the power of her mind. She imagined herself as being perfect, she concentrated her mind on giving her perfect contours, and a few years later, she was able to model bathing suits, so perfect had her body become. A motion picture was built around this amazing woman.

The power of mind that could cause man to change the very structure of his body, resides within the subconscious mind. We have studied this power elsewhere in this book. Through imagining the things that you want to happen to you, this power of creative mind is released in your body and in your life, and brings about the changes you desire.

Their Minds Grew Wings

Scientists wanted to test this power that exists in all living creatures. They took rose bushes, that a certain type of wingless parasite live on, and put them into a room, and submerged the bases of the pots in buckets of water. There was no way for the parasites to leave the rosebushes. Then the windows of the room were opened. In a few days time the parasites grew wings and flew out of their prison! So great is this power of resourcefulness and motivation in nature that it can cause the most amazing changes when necessity arises.

Another instance of how this secret power of the mind works, is that of six paralyzed male patients in a ward of a hospital in South America. The open window of this ward was near a jungle. One day a boa constrictor crawled up a tree and into the ward where these six helpless men lay on their beds. As the giant snake crawled towards them, all of these six men *got up from their beds and ran from the ward!* Despite the fact their muscles had not been used for years, they found the power, somehow, to stumble out of that ward, away from impending danger.

Medical books are full of such instances of miraculous cures. When the mind's and body's reserves of power are tapped under emotional excitation, the threat of danger, or the impetus of a powerful imagination, a person can often achieve amazing cures.

Cathedrals, Palaces and Skyscrapers

A creative idea, held in your mind, is as real as a cathedral, a palace or a skyscraper. The only thing that bridges the gap between dreams and ideas and their fulfilment in the outer world of reality, is the Dynamic Law of Action. In the fourth-dimensional realm of mind, all the great creations of man first flowered as ideas, dreams or thought-forms.

When we see a magnificent creation like St. Peter's Cathedral in Rome, or the Cathedral of Notre Dame in Paris, or St. Patrick's Cathedral in New York City, we do not see just blocks of granite, marble, stained glass windows and majestic towering ceilings covered with beautiful mosaics or brilliant paintings. We actually see the crystallized ideas and dreams of men who have had the daring and vision to dream magnificent dreams, and then, through the dynamic law of creative action, made those dreams come true.

Be Inspired by these Dreams

Study the pictures of these great masterpieces in art and architecture, and, if possible, see the originals in person. Let these artistic masterpieces inspire you to build your own mental rainbows, then follow them to the finding of the pot of gold at the end. Take as examples some of the world's most beautiful, tallest and most outstanding buildings, and let them serve as ideals by which you build your own temple of destiny.

The Taj Mahal is such a beautiful example. It is built of solid marble, and encrusted with semi-precious stones and inlaid with patinas of gold-leaf. This beautiful temple stands in the Kashmir Valley in India. It was built by an ancient ruler as a memorial to his wife.

Let this beautiful building become a memorial to the love that crowns your life with beauty and joy. Tap its inspirational power to make of your life a "temple, not a tavern."

Let your imagination soar to the lofty heights of the Empire State building in New York City. See its grandeur, its nobility, its aloofness, as it pierces the blue sky like a minaret, lifting its arms in silent meditation.

Emulate this Boldness and Courage

What boldness, what courage and imagination it took to conceive this tallest building in the world. Emulate the bold and courageous concept that made the creator of this edifice fight such discouraging odds in building it. The ability to overcome such formidable odds attests to the mental and moral fibre of men who dared dream big dreams and make them come true.

Let your mind conceive the dream first, then know that bold steps will lead you to the right actions to make your dream come true. Expand your consciousness into lofty realms; dare to dream big, dare to think big! Dare to search for the highest, the finest, the greatest, the most beautiful, the most idealistic, the most perfect, the richest, the grandest and the loftiest of all life's treasures. By holding these great concepts in your mind you will achieve the dazzling heights that these creations inspire.

Building Great Intellectual Power

Use this same process of emulation and study to build greater intellectual power. Add to your mental and emotional arsenal, the great concepts that have inspired the geniuses of all ages. Study the works of the leading philosophers, apply their precepts, their logic and wisdom, imitate their thoughts, and apply them to your own life.

Study the works and lives of such great minds as Plato, Socrates, Aristotle, Voltaire, Kant, and our modern Emerson, and any others you wish to add to your mental enjoyment and intellectual enrichment. Let their philosophy inspire you and lead you into fertile paths of original thinking and greater inspiration.

Then broaden your thinking to include the great thoughts of our most illustrious dramatists, authors and poets. Read the works of Shakespeare, study Milton and Dante, scan the works of the great Greek dramatists; read Ibsen, Shaw, and Wilde. Do not neglect our own great modern playwrights, O'Neill, Arthur Miller, William Inge, Edward Albee, Lillian Hellman, and Tennessee Williams. You should keep up to date in literature and drama and not scorn our modern authors, for often you will learn much from these modern playwrights. They reflect the thinking of our own age and show us the drama of human souls struggling with problems that are similar to our own.

Be Inspired by Nature's Grandeur

In expanding your mind and enlarging your concept of life, also be aware of and inspired by the natural grandeur that exists in the world.

When you stand in the presence of such natural wonders as the redwood trees in the Sequoia National Park, or Niagara Falls, Mt. Everest, the Grand Canyon of the Colorado, the Mississippi River, Death Valley, the Carlsbad Caverns, and other natural wonders that baffle the senses, you will ponder the mystery of life, the majesty and might of the intelligence in nature; the purpose and direction that all life takes under the propulsive power of a superior mind in nature, which man cannot even conceive.

When you become one with all these intelligence forces of nature, and build an awareness of the miracle which life presents to the senses, you will be in tune with the highest mental and spiritual forces in the universe.

Capture the Rhythm of Great Music

Many of life's mysteries will be revealed to you when your mind and emotions come under the sway of man's creative genius in all fields. You will be aware of your own inner, creative powers of mind; your perceptions will grow, your vision will soar, and your spirits will remain undaunted in the midst of life's greatest challenges. Your faith in yourself and in the invisible power back of all life will suddenly expand and cause you to do great things also. Capture the rhythm and beauty of great music from the geniuses of the past; Mozart, Chopin, Beethoven, Bach and Handel; these and other great composers of the past and present, can stir your mind and emotions into patterns of rhythm and harmony that will cause your soul to soar to lofty heights. There is power in music to uplift and inspire the mind of man. When you have once been exposed to the rhythm of the universal music of the spheres, and received the noble inspiration that great music gives the human consciousness, you will never be the same ordinary person. You will become extraordinary, illumined and raised to the lofty heights that these creative geniuses of history have scaled.

Think on these Great Things and Marvel

Think on these great things and marvel! Then go forth and create your own forms of creative greatness. Let them serve to inspire you to achieve great deeds. Let them be models for you to use for the achievement of perfection and beauty in your own life. Let these great events and inspired creations of the illumined minds of the past and present, awaken in your consciousness the awareness of your own Divinity.

The oak tree slumbers in the acorn. Your future greatness, your great achievement, your imprisoned splendour, slumber in your own immortal soul!